A TIME FOR CHAMPIONS
A ST. LOUIS SOCCER DYNASTY

A Time for Champions is the result of contributions from many talented individuals. Writers included Mikael Kriz, Tim Brassil, Patrick Murphy, Dan Leahy and Jim Murphy.

Editors included Terri Gates, Emily Haight, John Lindsay, Randy McGuire, Jason Peifer, Kay Porter, Alison Schutz and John Waide.

Publisher: Virginia Publishing

A Time for Champions is a publication of KETC/Channel 9, Jack Galmiche, President and CEO. Copyright 2010 by KETC/Channel 9

ISBN: 978-1-891442-55-1 • $49.95

Published for KETC/Channel 9 by Virginia Publishing Co. St. Louis, MO, www.STL-Books.com

Book designed by Ben Pierce, Virginia Publishing Co.

A TIME FOR CHAMPIONS book and documentary were a collaborative effort of KETC/Channel 9, Saint Louis University (SLU) and the Billiken Soccer Club (BSC). The book is the product of much effort on the part of a committee whose membership was derived from Channel 9, SLU and BSC. Some committee members were more involved than others but all contributed in some way. We wish to thank the members of Pius XII Memorial Library for their efforts in locating, editing and digitizing the hundreds of images required to create this pictorial history.

COMMITTEE MEMBERS:

CHANNEL 9: Jack Galmiche, John Lindsay, Patrick Murphy

SLU: Dr. Don Brennan, Kathy Luther, Mikael Kriz, John Waide, Dr. Randy McGuire, Jason Peifer, Dr. Bob Krizek, Dr. Paaige Turner, Mary Gould, Michael Lents, Doug McIlhaga, Brian Kunderman, James Jaramillo, Janet Oberle

BSC: Jim Murphy, Dan Leahy, Tim Brassil, Tom Mataya, Bill McDermott

In any book of this nature the selection of photos, as well as which players and opposing teams to mention, is a very subjective process. We therefore offer our apologies to anyone who may have been overlooked. Your contributions to the game and to the University that you represented are greatly appreciated.

Top: SLU Coach Bob Guelker. Bob Guelker holding the NCAA trophy high after the Billikens' win. (10 December 1965)

Bottom: SLU Billikens vs Sante Fe Reserves in Bogota, Colombia. The Billiken Soccer Team carries the Colombian flag prior to their match with the Sante Fe Reserves in Bogota, Colombia--the first stop on the 1973 South American Tour. Line of players on the left: Jim Bokern, Denny Werner, Dan Counce, Al Steck, Don Droege, Dan Flynn, and Kevin Handlan. Line of players on right: Bob Matteson, Pat Leahy, Chuck Zorumski, Bruce Hudson, Joe Clarke, Bruce Rudroff, Len Deschler, and John Roeslein (1973). *[Photographer unknown; original photo from SLU Sports Information Office]*

THANK YOU, FATHER LUKE

This book, its companion documentary, as well as many of the photos in the Saint Louis University yearbooks, would not have been possible if not for the photographic work of Father Luke. In many ways, this book shines a spotlight on the work Father Luke did with little recognition in his role as SLU's volunteer sports photographer.

Father Luke's real name was Boleslaus Thomas Lukaszewski. He was always referred to simply as 'Father Luke.' Boleslaus Thomas Lukaszewski was born on February 7, 1914, in Milwaukee, Wisconsin, where he was one of three sons. He attended Marquette High School in Milwaukee from 1928 to 1932. After graduating, he entered the Jesuits at St. Stanislaus Novitiate in Florissant, Missouri. He studied philosophy at SLU where he received his bachelor's degree in 1938 and his master's in 1940. Later in 1945, Father Luke was ordained a Catholic priest. Shortly thereafter he joined the philosophy faculty at SLU, where he served as an associate professor of philosophy for over 20 years until his death on March 22, 1970.

When SLU started its soccer program, the team was required by the University's health insurance policy to be accompanied on its trips by a full-time faculty member in order for the players to be covered in the event of injury or accident. Since neither Coach Guelker nor later Coach Keough were full time faculty members, Father Luke volunteered. An avid amateur photographer, Father Luke soon found himself at almost every University athletic event and social activity as SLU's unofficial photographer. He served in that capacity for over 20 years. Many of his University photographs were published in a pictorial history of SLU issued in 1968 to commemorate the University's 150th anniversary.

Some of the players remember Father Luke's fondness for participating in trivia and word games with the team to pass time on the bus trips out of town. Others believe he may have been the only person on the bus who actually could recite the Joyful or Glorious Mysteries when the team prayed the Rosary on its trips. But everyone remembers that he was always there to encourage and help the team in any way he could.

Father Luke, you have helped us once again by having shot a treasure trove of photographs through the years that enable us to tell our story. Thank you many times over.

Father Boleslaus Lukaszewski, SJ. Father Boleslaus Lukaszewski, SJ was known simply as "Father Luke" by his countless Saint Louis University friends. He attended most Billiken Soccer games to photograph the action and was a friend to all the players. Father Luke died on Palm Sunday of 1970, and his passing was mourned by the entire SLU community. (This *photo dates from 10 June 1959) [It may be a self-portrait by Father Luke.]*

INTRODUCTION

The light of American soccer shines brightly today. At its highest level, the U.S. Men's National Team has qualified for the 2010 World Cup hosted in South Africa. The National Team is consistently ranked among the International Federation of Association Football's (FIFA) top 20 teams of all the men's national teams in the world. It can now compete with the best, and on occasion can prevail, as it did in 2008 when it defeated Spain 2-0 in South Africa. Spain was then one of the top-ranked teams in the world.

At the professional level, Major League Soccer (MLS) is thriving. MLS now consists of 16 teams located throughout the United States. The Seattle franchise, in its second year of existence, has sold over 30,000 season tickets for 2010. At other levels, almost all colleges and high schools now field teams, both men's and women's. In addition, hundreds of thousands of young people participate in organized soccer across the United States. In fact,

soccer has become so mainstream that is has spurred a new generation of 'soccer moms.' Soccer has indeed fully arrived in the United States.

This has not always been the case. Some 50 years ago, soccer presented a vastly different picture in the U.S. There was little in the way of grassroots soccer being played. In most areas transplanted Europeans, Latin Americans and other ethnic groups made up the majority of participants in competition-level soccer in America. Prior to 1959, soccer was not even a sanctioned NCAA Division I sport. Organized youth soccer teams were hard to find. The men's national team was seldom competitive with the teams of other countries. There was one notable exception to the general malaise of soccer in America, and that was the soccer scene in St. Louis, Missouri.

St. Louis has long had a rich soccer heritage. Like all other soccer in the U.S., its origins in St. Louis were ethnically based. However, there were two differences in St. Louis that made soccer's success unique: the melting pot effect and the Catholic

Youth Council (CYC). The CYC was a mainstay in St. Louis on levels both social and athletic. Its widespread presence was largely attributed to the fact that in the 1950s St. Louis was about 50 percent Catholic. As for soccer specifically, the CYC, through its organized youth leagues, provided a "farm system" for men's soccer talent. Every parish in St. Louis had one or more teams in every age group participating. These soccer players were funneled into the many, mostly Catholic high schools that fielded soccer teams. The competition among those high school teams was fierce, as was the competition between CYC parish teams. The game was played at a very high level in the men's senior leagues. The Kutis and Simpkin teams were as successful as any team in the U.S. This was particularly evidenced by Kutis' record in the nationwide Amateur Cup and Open Cup competitions. From 1956 to 1961, Kutis won six consecutive Amateur Cup titles and in 1957 one Open Cup title.

The strength of St. Louis soccer was further supported by the creation of the famous Men's National Team which participated in the 1950 World Cup in Brazil. That team astonishingly upset number-one ranked England in that tournament 1-0 despite being composed of amateur, part-time players. Of the 11 starters on the U.S. team, five were from St. Louis - Harry Keough, Frank Borghi, Gino Pariani, Pee Wee Wallace and Charlie Colombo.

The 1950s saw an abundance of local soccer talent growing and thriving in St. Louis. Yet the number of outlets for this talent were limited. It wasn't until 1959 that this changed—the NCAA sanctioned men's soccer as a collegiate sport. Men's soccer finally became part of the college sports landscape and Saint Louis University was able to burst onto the college soccer scene due to the abundance of local talent. For the next 15 years, SLU soccer teams dominated Division I men's collegiate soccer in an unparalleled fashion, winning or sharing 10 NCAA championships.

This book is devoted to chronicling that era of excellence in Saint Louis University soccer. Please sit back and enjoy this amazing story.

A TIME FOR CHAMPIONS

This is the story of a time when a sport became more than a game. In America, soccer developed its own distinct style in East Coast cities. As the country moved west, so, too, did soccer – Americanized, aggressive, fast and tough.

In the rapidly growing industrial city of St. Louis, European immigrants played a raw, competitive style of the game in the city's working class, Roman Catholic neighborhoods.

It was a time for champions.

In 1874, St. Louis was the country's fourth largest city. Boosters called it, optimistically, the Paris of the Midwest. Its main thoroughfare was the Mississippi River, and its levee was jammed with steamboats carrying passengers and goods from every corner of the country.

Immigrants from Ireland, Germany, Italy and Eastern Europe sought jobs – and moved to St. Louis neighborhoods, bringing their languages, their religion — predominantly Catholic — and their favorite sport: soccer.

The sport fit well with the competitive spirit of European immigrants. And it was a cheap game to play, requiring little equipment, few rules and a vacant lot. Ethnic teams battled both on and off the field for bragging rights.

The St. Louis Archdiocese created through its Catholic Youth Council (CYC) perhaps the most highly organized soccer league of any American city. So neighborhood kids learned soccer as soon as they were old enough to kick a ball.

The local soccer culture produced players and teams that showed everyone Americans could play the world's sport.

Every four years, teams from around the world compete for the sport's greatest honor: the World Cup. In 1950 the American team that made the 30-hour plane trip to Brazil included five St. Louis players on the 11-man team. Four of the St. Louis players came from the same Italian neighborhood, which is known as

The Hill. If you grew up on The Hill during the Depression, two things were pretty certain: You were Italian, and you played a lot of sports.

But the challenge before them was daunting. They lost their first game in the tourney against Spain 3-1. Their next challenge would be England, a team many believed would win the World Cup. The American team had few illusions about the likely outcome. London bookmakers put the odds against an American World Cup victory at 500-to-1.

But America's defense held strong. And when the final whistle blew, thousands of spectators poured onto the field. It was the world's favorite story: little guy with heart— and luck — beats big guy.

In the late 1950s and early 1960s St. Louis was building the Mercury space capsules that would take the first men into space. The city was producing Corvettes to take Americans for a ride on the nation's new highways. And it was building the country's tallest monument – a stainless steel arch celebrating its role as the Gateway to the West. It was a city with the right stuff. And a new generation, from working-class roots, was heading to college.

For young St. Louis Catholics in the late 1950s, the logical school of choice would have been St. Louis University,

then a small Jesuit college. It was a commuter school, allowing students from blue-collar families to attend college and live at home.

It was their ticket to a better life, a chance to make a name for themselves. But as it turned out, they would make a name for the school as well.

Some sports teams are known as Tigers, Bulldogs or Bears. St. Louis University's mascot is the Billiken, a chubby, jovial elf believed to bring luck and good fortune. But it was more than luck that drove the St. Louis soccer Billikens to future championships.

Bob Guelker, executive director of the St. Louis CYC, had approached the University to volunteer his services as a coach. Guelker loved soccer, and though he'd never played it, was an avid student of tactics on the field.

In the Billikens' first year of varsity soccer, the program had a budget of two hundred dollars and no frills. They were unique among college teams in that they were all home town boys with something to prove — that their brand of soccer was better than anyone else's.

In 1959, the National Collegiate Athletic Association (NCAA) created Division I Soccer, offering colleges the opportunity to compete for a national title.

The NCAA championship game was played that year at the University

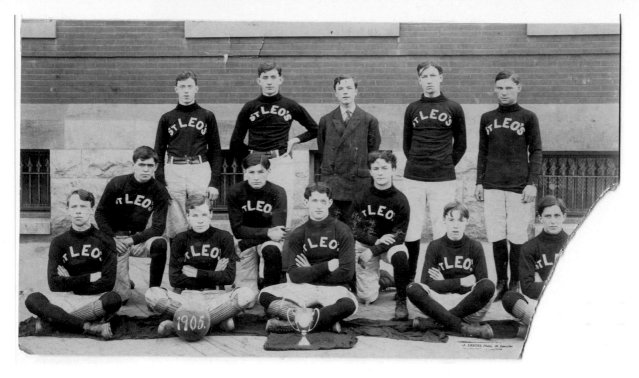

of Connecticut on a wet Thanksgiving weekend. This was the first full season for varsity soccer at St. Louis University. Sloshing toward the title, the Billikens beat the University of Bridgeport 5-2 for the national title. The first NCAA championship had been won by a Midwestern school, St. Louis University (SLU). And, with this win, SLU had placed an unusual story in the annals of sports. Soccer had joined the big leagues. And this first championship marked a turning point that was historic, showing colleges throughout America that soccer had been taken to a new level.

Having taken the championships in 1959, 1960, '62 and '63, the team had grown accustomed to victories. Guelker liked winning as much as his players, but he also wanted to promote the game across the country, and he knew that lopsided victories would not help anybody.

Coming into the '65 season there was cause for concern. Only four players with game action were returning from the past year. It would be a time for rebuilding at a point when other schools had begun recruiting St. Louis talent.

But the underclassmen surprised everyone. Raised in the local soccer culture, they stepped up and kicked their way to another national championship.

It was the seventh year of NCAA Division I Soccer. The Billikens had

made seven championship appearances, winning five. They were the undisputed national college soccer powerhouse.

In 1966, Bob Guelker left St. Louis University to head up a new soccer program at Southern Illinois University in Edwardsville, just across the river. It was the beginning of a new chapter – under a new coach — Harry Keough of World Cup fame. Harry was a player's coach. He knew what it was like out there on the field, and he knew that to win games, you needed more than good athletes. You needed the right players in the right positions and a strong sense of unity.

But by 1967, the landscape was changing. The number of college teams was growing, and with more schools recruiting St. Louis players, the field had grown more competitive.

Harry's first season was a tough one. But as the season progressed, the team adapted to the style and the expectations of their new coach and made it to the finals, facing off once again against rival Michigan

State. While college teams around the country were developing their programs by recruiting both St. Louis players and athletes from other countries, Keough continued Guelker's strategy of building the roster almost exclusively from neighborhood kids who had come up through the ranks of the CYC.

The team showed their competitors a style of soccer that relied on tight control of the ball and aggressive, highly coordinated, constant attacks on the opponent's goal. Keough's objective was to shape a team that was as mentally focused

as it was physically fit.

In 1969 the Billikens sailed through an undefeated season with no ties.

In the final they defeated San Francisco for the NCAA title.

They'd found their groove – motivated by the knowledge that they had a lot to live up to.

Over a period of 15 years St. Louis University had won 10 NCAA Division I Championships – five under Bob Guelker and five under Harry Keough. Both were inducted into the National Soccer Hall of Fame.

The Billikens became America's first college soccer dynasty, with a string of titles that has not been equaled since.

Through the 1960s and 1970s the homegrown teams of St. Louis University set the bar for collegiate soccer, creating a dynasty and spreading the popularity of the sport across the nation. But 1973 would be the last championship year for St. Louis.

Though future championships would elude St. Louis, it wasn't because of a decline in the quality of the team. Over the past 36 years, the Billikens

have won more than 70 percent of their games, qualified for all but five NCAA tournaments, and produced 48 All-Americans.

More teams with more scholarships to lure St. Louisans to play for them had raised the level of competition to the point that a single team could no longer dominate the sport. College soccer's gain might have been the Billikens' loss, but St. Louis was there first.

From its humble beginnings in city school yards and neighborhood parks, soccer has grown over the past 30 years into the nation's most popular organized sport among boys and girls across America.

Soccer is a simple game of kicking a ball into a net. But there is drama in the attack and determination in the defense.

It is a game of grace and grit.

And when we speak of its champions, their glory lies not in victory alone. It lives in the spirit that compels them, even against the odds, to find those moments in their lives that prove whoever they are, wherever they come from, they are the best.

Page 7: 1950 U.S. World Cup team in Brazil

Page 8 top: World Cup 1950 - the winning goal!

Page 8 bottom: Ben Miller's team. Teams representing the Ben W. Miller Hat Company of St. Louis won seven league titles and reached the U.S. Open Cup in 1926.

Page 9 top: St. Leo's soccer team, 1905. Comprised of members of the St. Leo's Sodality, a church men's organization, St. Leo's teams won nine consecutive championships beginning in 1905.

Page 9 bottom: Coach Bob Guelker, 1961

Page 10 left: An aerial view of the Saint Louis University campus, 1960

Page 10/11: SLU Billikens vs. Cleveland State at Musial Field in St. Louis. Billiken Jim Bokern scores on a penalty kick in a 4-1 SLU victory. (8 October 1972)

Page 11 top right: SLU team celebrates victory over UCLA in 1972.

Page 11 bottom right: SLU plays SIUE at Musial Field, 1969.

Page 12 top left: SLU Billiken John Pisani hangs suspended in the air after heading a goal against South Florida in 1968.

Page 12 top right: Coach Harry Keough with trophies, 1967

Page 12 bottom left: SLU plays at Musial Field with the unfinished Gateway Arch in the background, 1965.

Page 12 bottom right: SLU vs. Ball State (28 September 1963)

Page 13 top: Close-up of SLU vs Michigan State University at East Lansing, MI. Jerry Knobbe, the team captain, in action (17 October 1959) *[Photo by Father Luke]*

Page 13 middle: Coach Bob Guelker with his 1962 championship team in 1962.

Page 13 bottom: SLU plays SIUE in the second game of the 1973 NCAA Tournament.

Coach Bob Guelker holds up NCAA Trophy after SLU beat Michigan State 1-0 at Francis Field in 1965.

1958

1958 BILLIKENS SOCCER CLUB SCHEDULE

DATE	OPPONENT	NICKNAME	PLACE	SLU	OPPONENT
11 Oct.	Wheaton College	Crusaders	Fairgrounds Pk #1	1	1
25 Oct.	Kenrick Seminary		(Exhibition Game)	2	1
1 Nov.	Illinois	Fighting Illini	Fairgrounds Pk #1	5	1
29 Nov.	Midwest All-Stars	All-Stars	Pub. School Stadium	3	1

1958 SLU Soccer Club: Row 1 (L-R) - Bob Kaufman, Terry Malone, John Michalski and Dan Puricelli. **Row 2** - Mike Houlihan, Bob Guelker, Coach; Steve Murphy and Bill O'Brien, Captain; Larry King, Assistant Coach and Gene Block. **Row 3** - Bob Endler, Tom Quigley, Jim Monahan, Jack Dueker, Jerry Knobbe and John Fuchs. **Row 4** - Tom Richmond, Don Kelly, George Endler, Co-Captain; Bob Burns, Bob Malone and Lee Manna. Missing from the photo: Don Range and John Klein. *[Photo by Father Luke]*

MIDFIELD MEMORY:

1958'S PIVOTAL GAME

By Bill O'Brien

In 1958, SLU sponsored a club soccer team. The rationale for doing so was to determine whether or not the University should start a soccer program in 1959 when the NCAA made soccer a sanctioned varsity sport. The 1958 team played an abbreviated four-game season, winning three and tying one.

Nevertheless, the jury was still out at the University on whether to proceed with soccer in 1959. To convince the University to move forward, Coach Bob Guelker arranged for an exhibition game against a Midwest college all-star team after the college soccer season was completed.

The game was played on the Saturday after Thanksgiving in Fairgrounds Park, the municipal park that SLU used as its home field. The college all-stars arrived in St. Louis only to learn that snow had

blanketed the field. The morning of the game, students and fans swept the snow clear from the two penalty areas, leaving the rest of the field covered in snow. Several of the college all-stars were seen touching and tasting the snow. They were foreign players who, as the story goes, had never seen snow before.

So the game was played in winter weather, on a slippery and frozen field. It was SLU, with its all-St. Louis roster, against a team comprised of players from the University of Illinois,

Purdue, the University of Indiana and Michigan State. Michigan State had been undefeated for the last three years and was considered by many to be the "unofficial NCAA champion." SLU dominated the college all-stars, winning the game 5-0.

Looking back now, 52 years later, on the value of playing this Midwest college all-star team, one realizes how pivotal this game was to SLU's soccer program.

The solid 5-0 victory over this team of all-stars proved to friend and foe alike,

even the University's administration, that locally born and raised St. Louisans attending SLU were among the nation's best soccer players.

The crowd on that blustery, winter day was estimated to be a couple thousand spectators. It was a mix of students and local soccer fans. The size of the crowd in such inclement weather assured the University that there would be strong local fan support.

The victory over the Midwest college all-stars gave immediate credibility

to the 1959 SLU team. It helped Bob Guelker fill his first year's schedule with top-notch, competitive opponents. Without playing and beating such highly regarded opponents during the 1959 regular season, it's unlikely the Billikens would have been selected as the Midwest's representative to the NCAA Tournament in their first year.

Page 17 top: SLU Soccer Club vs Midwest All-Stars at Public School Stadium in St. Louis. George Endler gets control of the ball for SLU after a skirmish at midfield. Don Range looks on from the right rear and Lee Manna looks over his shoulder from the far right. (30 November 1958) *[Photo by Father Luke]*

Page 17 bottom: An All-Star goalie tries to block a SLU kick into the net at Public School Stadium. (30 November 1958) *[Photo by Father Luke]*

Page 18: SLU vs Midwest All-Stars. SLU players L-R are Bill O'Brien, George Endler, Don Range, Jerry Knobbe, John Michalski, Tom Richmond, Jack Dueker and John Fuchs. (30 November 1958) *[Photo by Father Luke]*

Page 19 top right: SLU Soccer Club vs Midwest All-Stars at Public School Stadium in St. Louis. SLU players (L-R): Jerry Knobbe running in from the left, Steve Murphy, and Don Kelly, who is struggling to keep his balance. (30 November 1958) *[Photo by Father Luke]*

Page 19 bottom right: SLU Soccer Club vs Midwest All-Stars at Public School Stadium in St. Louis. SLU players are (L-R): Beginning with George Endler, who has the ball, Don Range in center background, and John Fuchs and John Klein in the right background. (30 November 1958) *[Photo by Father Luke]*

Page 20 top: SLU Soccer Club vs Midwest All-Stars at Public School Stadium in St. Louis. A goal-to-goal view of the field. (30 November 1958) *[Photo by Father Luke]*

Page 20 bottom: SLU Soccer Club vs Midwest All-Stars at Public School Stadium in St. Louis. George Endler makes another attempt at the goal surrounded by All Star players. (30 November 1958) *[Photo by Father Luke]*

1959

1959 BILLIKENS SOCCER CLUB SCHEDULE

DATE	OPPONENT	NICKNAME	PLACE	SLU	OPPONENT
26 Sept.	Dayton Univ	Flyers	Dayton, OH	10	0
3 Oct.	Illinois	Fighting Illini	Champaign, IL	6	1
7 Oct.	MacMurray College	Highlanders	Fairgrounds Pk #1	11	1
11 Oct.	Indiana Univ	Hoosiers	Fairgrounds Pk #1	5	0
17 Oct.	Michigan State	Spartans	East Lansing, MI	4	2
24 Oct.	Univ of Chicago	Maroons	Fairgrounds Pk #1	6	0
31 Oct.	Navy Pier, UIC	Sailors	Fairgrounds Pk #1	8	0
7 Nov.	Wheaton College	Crusaders	Wheaton, IL	1	2
14 Nov.	Purdue Univ	Boilermakers	Lafayette, IN	5	0
NCAA Playoffs					
22 Nov.	Univ of San Francisco	Dons	Pub School Stadium	4	0
26 Nov.	City College of NY	Beavers	Storrs, CT	6	2
28 Nov.	Univ of Bridgeport	Purple Knights	Storrs, CT	5	2

1959 SLU Championship Soccer Team: Row 1 (L-R) - Gene Block, Bob Kauffman, Bill Mueller. **Row 2:** Bob Malone, Terry Malone, Tom Richmond, Pat Griffard. **Row 3:** Tom Trost, John Fuchs, Bob Pisoni, John Michalski, Captain Jerry Knobbe, Coach Bob Guelker. **Row 4:** John Klein, Bob Endler, George Endler, Jack Dueker, Tom Barry, Don Range.

On Friday, September 25, 1959, the Saint Louis University Billiken soccer team began its first season in collegiate soccer. That year, the team lost only one game en route to the very first NCAA soccer national title. The team amassed a total of 71 goals over 12 games, with 24 being scored by George Endler. A final 5-2 victory over the University of Bridgeport on November 28th in Storrs, Connecticut, gave SLU the national championship. This team was composed entirely of St. Louis players, most of whom came through the ranks of the CYC. The players were highly talented from years of playing organized soccer in an environment conducive to the sport. The first championship team featured three All-Ameicans: Jack Dueker, Jerry Knobbe and Tom Trost.

SIDELINE:
WHITE CLOUD

The photo at the right was taken in an airplane Billiken players affectionately nicknamed 'White Cloud.' For most of the players, their first airplane ride was on a soccer trip for SLU. For that reason White Cloud has a special place in the memories of almost every player. Every year, there would be an away game or two at such a distance that it required the Billikens to fly rather than take a bus to their destination. SLU would charter a plane for these trips with Interstate Airmotive Inc., located at the back end of Lambert Field. The plane used was normally a DC-3, a four-propeller plane.

Although each team has its own memories, trips to the Air Force Academy are frequently mentioned. It seems that White Cloud could easily arrive and land in Colorado Springs with the entire team and its baggage. Taking off, however, was a different matter! The plane could not take off fully loaded and clear the nearby Rocky Mountains for the return flight. Consequently, the pilot would fly the empty plane to Denver and the team would then ride a bus from the Air Force Academy in Colorado Springs to Denver, where it would board White Cloud for a safe journey home!

MIDFIELD MEMORY:

RECOLLECTIONS OF A GOALKEEPER

By Gene Block

My most vivid recollection of the 1959 season was the semifinal game in the NCAA Tournament. The game was played at the University of Connecticut at Storrs. Our opponent was City College of New York (CCNY). We had two starting players on the team who were not allowed to play in the tournament because of the NCAA's 10-semester rule. To make up for the two players we lost, Coach Guelker added two players to the team. One was Lee Manna, who played on the 1958 club team. He had not come out for the 1959 team because he had married and needed to work after school.

At halftime of the semifinal game, we were down 2-1, having scored our only goal about a minute before the end of the first half. When we went into the locker room, Lee Manna jumped up on a table in the middle of the room. He proceeded to tell us, "We aren't playing the St. Louis brand of soccer! We didn't fly all the way from St. Louis to lose the first game and have to turn around and fly back home!" I think he stunned us all with his forceful speech. Suddenly someone knocked on the door and said it was time for the second half to start. We went back out onto the field without Coach Guelker having said one word to the team.

It must have worked because in the second half we scored five goals to win the semifinal game 6-2. That put us into the championship game two days later, which we won 5-2. In all the years I played competitive sports, I have never heard a better motivational talk than Lee's.

In that semifinal game I believe Lee was the star of the game, and the irony was he didn't even get into the game.

SIDELINE:

HOME FIELD ADVANTAGE IS A STATE OF MIND!

In keeping with the Jesuit tradition of frugal fiscal policy, SLU did not invest in

a game field on campus for the first six years of the soccer program. So the soccer Bills initially played regular season home games in public parks.

The picture in the top right was taken at Fairgrounds Park, considered the home field for the soccer Bills for the first five years. The City of St. Louis put up a tarpaulin on the fence around the field, known as Fairgrounds #1 by the Parks Department. The tarped fence enabled SLU to charge admission for its home games: $1 for adults and $0.75 for students. Many fans will remember the

Andy Frain ushers who worked the ticket booths and maintained security.

In 1964, some of the home games were moved to Mullaly Field, the playing field for St. Mary Magdalene Parish. In 1965, SLU opened Musial Field, its first on-campus home field. Of course, the fiscally conservative Jesuits did not bring in topsoil or turf to landscape the field. Rather, they simply lined a vacant lot and put up goal posts. Many of the players in the first season suffered sprained ankles from stepping on pieces of buried bricks and other material left over

from the demolition of the former Mill Creek development. The coach from the University of British Columbia threatened to cancel his team's game against the Bills after seeing the poor condition of the turf in the pre-game warm up. Perhaps he should have, as his talented team lost the game to the Bills. After his team's 1966 loss at Musial Field, Gene Kenney, former coach of Michigan State University, called it, "The worst ever. No one should be subjected to playing on that field."

The condition of Musial Field stands in stark contrast to that of present day Hermann Stadium field, as well as SLU's adjacent practice field. These fields are first-class, with smooth, grass turf surfaces.

For the finals of the NCAA Tournaments, as well as a few other special games, the Billikens played at two well-known stadiums in the St. Louis area. In 1961, Public School Stadium was the site of the first ever St. Louis-hosted NCAA final. Francis Field, Washington University's football stadium was the site of the NCAA finals in 1962, 1965 and 1967 as well as a game against the U.S. Olympic team in 1963.

SIDELINE:

ST. LOUIS VS THE WORLD

A common thread of the SLU soccer competition against other colleges in the early years was that while the SLU teams were made up of homegrown St. Louis area talent, the other schools' teams were composed of many international players. This fact is well illustrated by the roster of SLU's very first intercollegiate opponent, Dayton University, in the game that was played on September 25, 1959, in Dayton, Ohio. Dayton's team consisted of players from Colombia, Peru, Mexico, Aruba, Greece and Germany. Dayton's coach was from Switzerland.

This difference in team composition created a continuing dynamic tension to SLU's soccer competition. The foreign-born players on other teams were often more individually skilled than the SLU players and had a condescending attitude toward American players. However, a few talented individuals do not necessarily make up a good team. The SLU teams were usually able to win the game over those teams by relying on superior fitness, extra effort and teamwork. The maxim that the "whole can be greater than the sum of its parts" was once again demonstrated by the success of those SLU teams. By the way, SLU beat Dayton in that inaugural game 10-0.

Page 22 bottom: SLU vs Michigan State University at East Lansing, MI. Don Range (in dark jersey on left) marks a Michigan State attacker as Bob Malone comes over to help. (17 October 1959) *[Photo by Father Luke]*

Page 23 bottom: SLU Billikens vs Chicago University at Fairgrounds Park #1 in St. Louis. John Klein (#20) dribbles past Chicago defenders as (L-R) Don Range, George Endler and Bob Kauffman watch. (24 October 1959) *[Photo by Father Luke]*

Page 24 top right: SLU vs Michigan State University at East Lansing, MI. Bob Malone (on left) approaches the ball with George Endler and Don Range (L-R) alongside. Tom Trost (far right) plays the wing position. (17 October 1959) *[Photo by Father Luke]*

Page 24 bottom left: SLU Billikens vs Chicago University at St. Louis Fairgrounds Park #1. SLU's Bob Pisoni hovers over the ball as teammate Bob Malone (on right) watches. (24 October 1959) *[Photo by Father Luke]*

Page 25 top: Victorious Billiken Soccer Players celebrate on their chartered plane, the "White Cloud," after defeating the Michigan State Spartans, 4-2. (17 October 1959) The players are (L-R), 1st row, Don Range, Jerry Knobbe and Bob Kauffman. 2nd row, Gene Block, John Michalski, Pat Griffard, George Endler and Tom Trost. 3rd row, Jack Dueker, Tom Barry, Bill Mueller, Bob Pisoni, Coach Bob Guelker, Bob Malone and John Fuchs. *[This image was published in the 23 October 1959 University News, page 13, and in the 1960 Archive yearbook, page 92. It was probably taken by Father Luke but is not found among his photos.]*

Page 25 bottom: SLU Billikens vs Chicago University at St. Louis Fairgrounds Park #1. The Billikens score on Chicago in a 6-0 victory. SLU Players (L-R): Bob Pisoni, George Endler and Tom Trost on the ground. Future Billikens Joe Westhus and Jim Murphy in crowd. See sideline page 31. (24 October 1959) *[Photo by Father Luke]*

Page 26 top: SLU Billikens vs Chicago University at Fairgrounds Park #1 in St. Louis. SLU All-American, Bob Malone, works the ball flawlessly through his Chicago University opponents. (24 October 1959) *[Photo by Father Luke]*

Page 26 middle: SLU Billikens vs Chicago University at St. Louis Fairgrounds Park #1. John Michalski (in glasses) dribbles the ball downfield with Tom Trost and Jack Dueker to his left and John Klein to his right. (24 October 1959) *[Photo by Father Luke]*

Page 27 top: Close-up of SLU Billikens vs Navy Pier in St. Louis at Fairgrounds Park #1. SLU's George Endler and a Navy Pier defender battle for the ball while Billikens Tom Trost (left) and Terry Malone (right) track with the play. (31 October 1959) *[Photo by Father Luke]*

Page 27 bottom: NCAA Playoff, Quarter Finals, SLU Billikens vs San Francisco at Public School Stadium in St. Louis. All-American, Tom Trost, settles the ball while George Endler (middle) and Terry Malone (top of picture) look on. (22 November 1959) *[Photo by Father Luke]*

Page 28 top: NCAA Playoff, Quarter Finals, SLU Billikens vs San Francisco at Public School Stadium in St. Louis. Billikens attack San Francisco's goal. SLU players (L-R): Tom Barry (#15), Tom Trost (#7), Don Range and Jack Dueker (#19). (22 November 1959) *[Photo by Father Luke]*

1960

1960 BILLIKENS SOCCER CLUB SCHEDULE

DATE	OPPONENT	NICKNAME	PLACE	SLU	OPPONENT
17 Sept.	Farleigh-Dickinson	Knights	Madison, NJ	2	3
24 Sept.	Wheaton College	Crusaders	Fairgrounds Pk #1	4	0
1 Oct.	Illinois	Fighting Illini	Champaign, IL	3	0
8 Oct.	Indiana Univ	Hoosiers	Bloomington, IN	12	0
11 Oct.	Washington Univ	Bears	Fairgrounds Pk #1	5	1
15 Oct.	Michigan State	Spartans	Fairgrounds Pk #1	4	0
22 Oct.	Pittsburgh	Panthers	Fairgrounds Pk #1	4	0
28 Oct.	Air Force Academy	Falcons	Colorado Springs, CO	3	1
5 Nov.	Navy Pier, UIC	Sailors	Chicago, IL	2	0
6 Nov.	Univ of Chicago	Maroons	Chicago, IL	10	0
12 Nov.	Purdue Univ	Boilermakers	Fairgrounds Pk #1	12	0
18 Nov.	Akron Univ	Zips	Fairgrounds Pk #1	5	3
NCAA Playoffs					
21 Nov.	Univ of California	Golden Bears	Pub. School Stadium	2	0
25 Nov.	West Chester	Golden Rams	Brooklyn, NY	2	1
26 Nov.	Univ of Maryland	Terrapins	Brooklyn, NY	3	2

In 1960, the Billikens lost their first match of the season to Farleigh-Dickinson University, 3-2. The team, however, recovered and dominated the rest of the season, outscoring their opponents 71-11. The Billikens won their second, and the NCAA's second, national soccer championship. Gerry Balassi led the team in scoring 19 goals and John Klein received All-American honors. The team was developing a high profile and their visibility in the St. Louis community was growing.

A major reason for the increased visibility was the significant newspaper coverage the Billikens received from the two major St. Louis newspapers, the *St. Louis Post-Dispatch* and the *St. Louis Globe-Democrat*. Each of those newspapers employed knowledgeable, full-time reporters who covered soccer. The *Post* reporter was Dent McSkimming and the *Globe-Democrat*'s was Charlie Gould. In 1961, Harold Flachsbart succeeded McSkimming as the *Post* reporter. It was not unusual at the time for both the *Post* and the *Globe-Democrat* to feature daily articles and photos about the soccer Billikens. A side benefit SLU received from this broad coverage was the large fan attendance at SLU home games. There were often crowds of a thousand or more fans in attendance.

1960 SLU Championship Soccer Team: Row 1 (L-R) - John Michalski, Tom McDonnell, Bob Trigg, John Winecoff, Pat Griffard, Student Manager Kim Tucci. **Row 2:** Mike Shanahan, Tom Hennessy, Bill Mueller, Mike Quinn, Tom Klein, Dick Werley. **Row 3:** Assistant Coach & Trainer Ed Quigley, Tom Richmond, Bob Malone, Ed Oswald, Gerry Balassi, Tony Tieber, John Klein, Tom Barry, Coach Bob Guelker. Missing: Don Range. *[Photo by Father Luke]*

SIDELINE:

SLU'S BUILT-IN FARM SYSTEM

If you look closely at the spectators to the side of the goal in the photo on page 25, you'll see Joe Westhus and Jim Murphy as eighth-graders playing for the Carondelet Sunday Morning Athletic Club. Here they are watching the Billikens play in Fairgrounds Park after their Khoury League game was over. This was not unusual, as most grade school and high school players aspired to one day play for the Bills.

In the early years of their soccer program, SLU could have been characterized as a 'local commuter

college,' as it drew the majority of its students from the Greater St. Louis Area. During this same period, amateur soccer in the city of St. Louis continued to flourish and build on the city's long-standing reputation as the premier soccer area in the U.S. Annually, teams from St. Louis competed for, and frequently won, national titles in the U.S. Open Cup, the U.S. Amateur Cup, and the National Junior Cup competitions. The Catholic Youth Council's (CYC) senior and junior programs, the Muny League and the Khoury League were widely regarded as among the best amateur soccer programs in the country. Consequently, it seemed only natural that almost all the players during the Bob Guelker era were native St. Louisans. Most had played for one of the many Catholic high schools in the area. Many were considered the stars of their CYC, Muny League or Khoury League teams. When the NCAA first sanctioned soccer as a varsity sport in 1959, Coach Guelker was able to pick his SLU team

from this pool of talented, local soccer players who were then attending SLU. In contrast, most other universities who fielded competitive soccer teams during the Bob Guelker era mainly drew their players from their pool of international students, or they recruited older, foreign athletes.

As the former coach of the St. Louis Prep Seminary soccer team, Bob Guelker had coached against most St. Louis-area high school soccer teams and as a result had seen many of the players in action. By the time he headed to SLU's soccer program, he was familiar with the players—former competitors now representing SLU. He also sought the input of local high school soccer coaches with respect to the talent and character of the players who were enrolling at SLU each year. In addition, as executive secretary of the CYC, almost all the coaches of the local CYC amateur soccer teams knew Coach Guelker and could provide him with their evaluations of players going into SLU. Now that's a farm system!

Page 31 bottom: Close-up of SLU Billikens vs Purdue University at Fairgrounds Park #1 in St. Louis. Tom Richmond (#3) and Tom Barry (#4) simultaneously leap to head the ball.

Page 32 top: SLU Billikens vs Wheaton at Fairgrounds Park #1 in St. Louis. Bob Malone (on ball) leads a Billiken offensive. SLU players, from foreground to background: Gerry Balassi (#5), Don Range (#10), Bob Trigg (#18), Tom Richmond and Tom McDonnell. (24 September 1960) *[Photo by Father Luke]*

Page 33 top: SLU Billikens vs Wheaton at Fairgrounds Park #1 in St. Louis. Tom Richmond traps the ball as teammates watch, L-R: Don Range (#10), John Michalski (#9) and Tom Klein. (24 September 1960) *[Photo by Father Luke]*

Page 33 bottom: Close-up of SLU Billikens vs Michigan State at Fairgrounds Park #1 in St. Louis. Gerry Balassi (#5) and Don Range (right) work together to keep the ball from Michigan State. (15 October 1960) *[Photo by Father Luke]*

Page 34 top left: Close-up of SLU Billikens vs Michigan State at Fairgrounds Park #1 in St. Louis. Bob Trigg and a Michigan State player clash over

the ball as Gerry Balassi looks back. (15 October 1960) *[Photo by Father Luke]*

Page 34 middle left: SLU Billikens vs Purdue University at Fairgrounds Park #1 in St. Louis. Gerry Balassi and a Purdue player battle for the ball. (12 November 1960) *[Photo by Father Luke]*

Page 35: Close-up of SLU Billikens vs Michigan State at Fairgrounds Park #1 in St. Louis. The

Billikens celebrate a goal. Listed L-R: Gerry Balassi, Mike Shanahan, Don Range, Bob Malone, John Michalski (#9), Tom McDonnell, Tom Richmond, Bob Trigg, John Klein, and Tom Hennessy. (15 October 1960) *[Photo by Father Luke]*

Page 36: 1960 NCAA Soccer Champs return to Saint Louis on a TWA Flight from Brooklyn, New York, where they defeated the University

of Maryland in the Second Annual NCAA Soccer Tournament. Pictured front to back: Coach Bob Guelker (carrying the trophy), Gerry Balassi, Co-Captain Don Range and John Klein. (26 November 1960) *[Photo by Father Luke]*

1961

1961 BILLIKENS SOCCER CLUB SCHEDULE

DATE	OPPONENT	NICKNAME	PLACE	SLU	OPPONENT
23 Sept.	Navy Pier, UIC	Sailors	Field No. 2 Forest Park	4	1
30 Sept.	Akron Univ	Zips	Akron, OH	2	3
8 Oct.	Illinois	Fighting Illini	Fairgrounds Pk. #1	4	0
12 Oct.	Washington Univ	Bears	Musial Field	4	3
14 Oct.	Indiana Univ	Hoosiers	Musial Field	8	1
21 Oct.	Indiana Tech	Warriors	Musial Field	12	0
25 Oct.	Pittsburgh	Panthers	Pittsburgh, PA	4	0
28 Oct.	Air Force Academy	Falcons	Musial Field	4	1
4 Nov.	Wheaton College	Crusaders	Wheaton, IL	2	0
5 Nov.	Univ of Chicago	Maroons	Chicago, IL	10	1
11 Nov.	Michigan State	Spartans	E. Lansing, MI	1	0
15 Nov.	Akron Univ	Zips	Musial Field	7	2
18 Nov.	Univ of San Francisco	Dons	San Francisco, CA	1	0
23 Nov.	Rutgers	Scarlet Knights	St. Louis, MO	6	1
25 Nov.	West Chester	Golden Rams	St. Louis, MO	0	2

1961 saw the men's soccer team lose their first national championship. Despite outscoring their opponents by a margin of well over 4-1 during the season, they lost the final to West Chester University 2-0. For the third year in a row, the Billikens made their way to the national championship game. Even if 1961 did not end the way the team had hoped, they were still the most impressive program in the country. Gerry Balassi again led the team in scoring with 17 goals and was named to the All-American team along with Bob Malone.

1961 SLU Soccer Team. Row 1 (L-R): Tony Tieber, Tom Barry, Pat Griffard, Ed Oswald, Jim Wiley, Rudy Kaschner, Gerry Balassi. **Row 2:** Assistant Coach Ed Quigley, Bill Mueller, Al Toczylowski, John Michalski, Bob Malone, Bob Trigg, Joe Hennessey, Tom Klein, Roger Rupp. **Row 3:** Coach Bob Guelker, Dave Robben, Bill Veith, Tom Hennessey, Mike Moore, Larry Cronin, Jim Bryon, Fred Boyd, Assistant Trainer Kim Tucci. *[Image published in 1962 Archive yearbook, page 104. Photo by Father Luke]*

SIDELINE:

WHO NEEDS SOCCER SCHOLARSHIPS? WE GET LUNCH MONEY!

Although there were no soccer scholarships at SLU until the late 1960s, the players did receive $.50 per day credit for lunch in the Griesedieck Hall dormitory cafeteria during the season. The credit was available Monday through Friday during the season only. A typical $0.50 lunch in the mid-sixties consisted of a roast beef sandwich on french bread, french fries, and a Coke.

Page 38 bottom: SLU Billikens vs Akron Zips in Akron, OH. SLU's Gerry Balassi maintains his balance as the ball goes out of play. (30 September 1961)

Page 39 bottom: SLU Billikens vs University of Illinois. SLU Joe Hennessey heads the ball, as teammates (L-R) Tom Barry, Gerry Balassi, and Bob Trigg are ready to help out. (8 October 1961) *[Photo by Father Luke]*

Page 40 top: SLU Billikens vs.Westchester State College Rams in the final NCAA Tournament at St. Louis. Bob Malone (#8) takes a desperate shot at the net through a crowded field of Rams defenders as Tom Klein (#16) looks on from the left. (25 November 1961) *[Photo by Father Luke]*

Page 40 bottom: SLU Billikens vs. Rutgers, NCAA Tournament. SLU's Bob Trigg battles for the ball

in the mud puddle as Rudy Kaschner (on right) supports the play. (23 November 1961)

Page 41 top: SLU Billikens vs. Michigan State. SLU player Pat Griffard (#6) fights for the ball as Bob Trigg (center) and Bill Vieth (right) look on. (11 November 1961) *[Photo by Father Luke]*

Page 41 bottom: SLU Billikens vs. Michigan State. SLU players L-R: Tom Barry, Gerry Galassi, Bob Malone, Al Toczylowski, Bill Vieth, Tom Klein. (11 November 1961) *[Photo by Father Luke]*

Page 42 top: SLU Billikens vs. Rutgers, NCAA Tournament. Billiken players catch their breath during halftime, listed L-R: Tony Tieber, Ed Oswald, Tom Klein, Rudy Kaschner, Fred Boyd (#23), Tom Barry, unidentified (in hooded jacket), and Bob Malone. (23 November 1961)

Page 43 top: SLU Billikens vs.Westchester. SLU's Bob Malone heads the ball between two Westchester defenders, surrounded by teammates (L-R) Bill Vieth, Tom Barry, and Bob Trigg. (25 November 1961) *[Photo by Father Luke]*

Page 43 bottom: SLU Billikens vs.West Chester. The Billikens put pressure on West Chester's goalie; SLU players L-R: Gerry Balassi (#5), Bob Malone, Tom Klein, Tom Barry. (25 November 1961) *[Photo by Father Luke]*

Page 44: Booters Close Season With Second Place Finish, The University News (December 1, 1961)

Kansas and Games

LUTZ

Bills play host State tomorrow 1-62 season gets uditorium will be opener's action. cheduled for 8:30

John Benington himself definite starters, but said pretty good idea" be. Mentioned as were Tom Kief-Harris (6'1) and ich (5'11) as Nordmann (6'7) d (6'4) as forarrison (6'8) as

NALISTS

the Bills are the of Coach Jim r the Jacks came th a 21-6 record. CAA tournament won the North e Title five times ears, and for the in a row. The lso averaged 80 last year, as ops' 69.7.

ed for their runfour of their top m last year, in-Terry Slattery, tage center, and o earned a 54.8 age. In the Bills hat they whipped 1-55, after Iowa from South Da-

MONDAY

e Bills head for Kansas in what game of the teams. Kansas last season, and up another winyear. In the past sas has compiled with a .637 win-After the loss of ars on the team, self at a disade height coming nced sophomores. ading scorer on ar, Wayne High-be playing with ior year. The loss all-Big 8 cage to Kansas strat-lightower placed ffensive play.

ATE NEXT

he Bills will be et Kansas State. Wildcats regard toughest oppo-and are sure to before they let inned. The Cats, er coach-of-the-(who has never ason), have lost eterans between te cagers, how-e edge over the eight, with 7'0 d 6'8 Joe Gottters.

hould be one of onents the Billi-this year. They number one in olls as compared placed sixteenth.

that the game is in the same with Cincinnati CAA Champs in rs.

rame, starting at tlight the inter-basketball game. y Means has his rter in forward with the first-to include: Rich uchowski as for-and Bill Lacey as going as center, ms reserve. The eature as guards e Gegg and Mike d Walker teams rter in forward

THE 1961 BILLIKEN NCAA RUNNER UP. 1st Row: (left to right Tony Tieber, Tom Barry, Pat Griffard, Ed Oswald, Jim Wiley, Rudy Kaschner, Gerry Balassi. 2nd Row: Ed Quigley (Asst. Coach) Bill Mueller, Al Toczlowski, John Michalski, Bob Malone, Bob Trigg, Joe Hennessey, Tom Klein, and Roger Rupp. 3rd Row: Coach Bob Guelker, Dave Robben, Bill Vieth, Tom Hennessey, Mike Moore, Larry Cronin, Jim Bryon, Fred Boyd, and Trainer Kim Tucci. Absent are: Al Klein, Tom McDonnell and Tom Dix.

Booters Close Season With Second-Place Finish In NCAA Tournament; Put Eight Players On Midwest League All-Star Team

By NOEL ABKEMEIER

The NCAA soccer tournament presented Billiken backers with unmatched excitement if not the ultimate victory that was hoped for. The defeat was then somewhat brightened by the naming of eight Billikens to the Midwest collegiate Soccer Conference All-Star Team.

Saturday's 2-0 defeat at the hands of West Chester (Pa.) State College, which dethroned the Bills after two years as champs, was the first defeat dealt the Bills in NCAA playoff competition and the first shutout in the four-year history of soccer at St. Louis U. As the score well indicates, West Chester set up a tight defense which disallowed the Bills the short shots which they generally set up. The Bills, however, still took their shots from a longer range but were thwarted by the outstanding play of John Juenger. The Billiken defense was not outshone as it held the Rams scoreless for over three periods and limited them to 17 shots while the Bills took 23.

Both scores came in the fourth period, the icebreaker coming on a 35 yard shot by inside left Bill Fulk after a pass from Ray Chil-lano on a foul kick. The final goal was scored from a similar distance by Joe Brownholtz with about ten minutes remaining.

MISSED PENALTY

A very important shot which could have been the turning point of the game was a missed penalty kick by Gerry Balassi early in the fourth quarter. Balassi, who played one of his best games, lofted the ball over the crossbar, a miss which was soon followed by the tie-breaking goal.

The Bills were not without other scoring opportunities, however, as they missed many scoring chances. Coach Bob Guelker said, "We had our chances in the first and third periods with the wind at our backs, but we couldn't get the finishing shot." This is backed up by the statistics which show 11 corner kicks for the Bills to only two for the Rams in addition to the Bills' outshooting them.

The result of the game was surprising considering the showings of both teams in Thursday's semifinal games. Thursday the Bills were at their unmatchable best, especially in the second half, as they handed Rutgers its first defeat of the season, 6-1. In contrast, West Chester made a poor showing in nosing out a struggling

Bridgeport eleven by a score of 2-0.

The final game left the Bills with a 13-2 mark for the season while West Chester went undefeated through its thirteen game slate.

EIGHT ALL STARS

Although the final game loss stole some of the hoped for team glory, individual honors were received as eight Billikens were named to the first team of the Midwest Collegiate Soccer Conference All-Star Team with a ninth player receiving honorable mention.

The first team included four forwards, two halfbacks, a fullback and the goalie from the Bills' conference champion team. The forward selections were led by high scoring outside right Gerry Balassi who led the Bills with 17 goals while adding nine assists. His most important goals came in the 1-0 triumphs over Michigan State and San Francisco.

Also selected was center forward Bob Trigg who broke up many a defense while ranking second in both goals and assists with 14 and 11 respectively for the season. Tony Tieber, tops in assists with 12 and fifth in goals with five, filled the outside left spot. Inside left Bob Malone, with six goals and eight assists, is the fourth Billiken on the forward line.

ROBBEN PICKED

Left halfback Bill Vieth, center halfback John Michalski and right fullback Joe Hennessey represented the Billiken defense on the conference team. Goalie Dave Robben tied with Ted Saunders of Michigan State for conference honors. Robben had six shutouts to his credit and also held the opposition scoreless in other games before

being removed.

Inside right Tom Klein of the Bills received honorable mention on the team. Klein ranked third in scoring with 13 goals and fifth in assists with seven. He scored three goals each against Akron and Rutgers in the NCAA playoff games.

SIX RETURNING

This marks the second straight season in which Michalski, Malone, Balassi and Trigg have re-:ceived conference honors. Of the Bills receiving recognition Michalski, Malone and Tieber are seniors; Balassi, Trigg, Vieth and Klein are juniors; and Robben and Hennessey are sophomores. Therefore, prospects for next year look very good with these six sophomores and juniors returning and the hope for return of injured Tom Hennessey and Tom McDonnell, both of whom were All-Conference in 1960.

Harry Caray To Cover Billiken Games On Radio

Fans can follow the basketball Billikens on radio again this season as Harry Caray resumes his familiar post as sports broadcaster for the Bills, assisted by one of last year's regulars, Gordy Hartweger, now serving as assistant freshman coach.

Broadcasts can be heard over WIL (1430 kc.) and KMOX (1120 kc.). WIL will carry the South Dakota game, while the Kansas, Kansas State and Kentucky games will be broadcast by KMOX.

Cross Country Ends Successful Season With 10-1 Record

After playing second fiddle to the soccer team for two years, Coach Gene Hart's cross country team has finally equaled it in success although not in fame. This season's 10-1 record in dual meet competition brought the harriers' three season total to 22-4 in contrast to the kickers' marks of 13-2 and 38-4.

The most recent encounter was the Central Collegiate Meet in Chicago where the Bills finished ninth in a field of fourteen teams. In this meet, the Bills' weakest showing of the year, Ashley finished 20th and Virdure 30th in a field of 71 runners.

In the other two invitational meets which the Bills entered this year they garnered first and second place honors. The first cross country trophy in the history of the school came to the Bills as they won the Quincy Invitational Meet. The second place finish came in the Missouri Valley Conference Meet on the Billikens' first try. These victories, coupled with the 10-1 record in dual meets, more than satisfied Coach Hart who said, "This great success for a team which is operating on a full scale basis for the first time this year."

ASHLEY LEADS

The success of the team is greatly due to the consistently fast running of Dick Ashley and Aaron Virdure. In the eleven dual meets Ashley was credited with ten first place finishes and one second place finish for a total of 12 points out of a possible minimum of 11. The sole second place was against Southeast Missouri State, a setback which was avenged in a later rematch. Ashley also finished fifth in the MVC meet to lead the Bills.

Virdure always finished close on Ashley's heels with a record of six second place finishes and five third place finishes for a total of 27 points. He added a seventh in the MVC meet.

In the only All-Freshman meet of the year, the MVC Postal Meet, the Bills placed well although not entering a full team in the competition. In the meet run over a two mile course Bob Willie finished 11th with a time of 10:48, Vic Nettle 13th in 10:59 and John Fischer 17th in 11:24. This did not count as a team entry since five men are needed for a full team.

1962

In 1962, the team returned only four starters from the previous year. However, this edition of the Billiken team featured the first undefeated season as they went 12-0-1. SLU's only tie that year came in their second game of the season against Notre Dame with a final score of 3-3. Soon after, the team began to gel and the goals poured in. The final game featured a shootout with the 1960 national title game opponent Maryland. Yet again, the Billikens defeated the Terrapins, this time 4-3 to win their third national championship. Again, Gerry Balassi led the scoring, this time with 16 goals, and Gerry received All-American honors along with Bill Vieth.

1962 BILLIKENS SOCCER CLUB SCHEDULE

DATE	OPPONENT	NICKNAME	PLACE	SLU	OPPONENT
29 Sept.	Indiana Univ	Hoosiers	Bloomington, IN	6	1
6 Oct.	Notre Dame	Fighting Irish	South Bend, IN	3	3
10 Oct.	Harris Teachers	Hornets	Musial Field	2	1
13 Oct.	Navy Pier, UIC	Sailors	Chicago, IL	6	1
17 Oct.	Indiana Tech	Warriors	Fort Wayne, IN	14	0
20 Oct.	Illinois	Fighting Illini	Musial Field	7	0
25 Oct.	Washington Univ	Bears	Musial Field	2	1
27 Oct.	Univ of Chicago	Maroons	Musial Field	13	0
3 Nov.	Wheaton College	Crusaders	Musial Field	3	0
10 Nov.	Michigan State	Spartans	Musial Field	2	1
17 Nov.	Stanford	Cardinals	Fairgrounds Pk. #1	9	3
22 Nov.	Michigan State	Spartans	Francis Field, MO	2	0
24 Nov.	Univ of Maryland	Terrapins	Francis Field, MO	4	3

1962 SLU Championship Soccer Team. Row 1 (L-R): Paul Garnier, John Butler, Ed Oswald, Roger Rupp, Fred Boyd, Larry Cronin, Tom Klein. **Row 2:** Co-captain Bill Vieth, James Rick, Don Ceresia, Al Toczylowski, Jim Byron, Joe Hennessy, Mike Moore, Gerald Schwalbe. **Row 3:** Trainer Kim Tucci, Ray Mann, Terry Knox, Tim Knox, Dan Leahy, Tom McDonnell, Co-captain Gerry Balassi, Tom Mataya, Coach Bob Guelker, Manager Bill Welsch. Missing from picture: Bob Trigg and Assistant Coach Tom Trost. *[Photo by Father Luke]*

Page 46 top: SLU Billikens vs Michigan State. All-American Don Ceresia shoots from midfield. (20 November 1962) *[Photo by Father Luke]*

Page 47 bottom: SLU Billikens vs Michigan State. SLU's Joe Henessey stretches to block a Michigan State shot as (L-R) Dan Leahy and Bill Vieth are poised to follow the action. (20 November 1962) *[Photo by Father Luke]*

Page 48 top: SLU Billikens vs Michigan State. SLU's Dan Leahy dribbles the ball around a Michigan State defender as Tom Klein (on left) rushes in and Tom Mataya (middle) looks on. (20 November 1962) *[Photo by Father Luke]*

Page 48 bottom: SLU Billikens vs Michigan State. SLU's Tom McDonnell (#13) and Tom Klein charge the ball as

Dan Leahy (in background) watches. (10 November 1962) *[Photo by Father Luke]*

Page 49 top: NCAA Tournament, SLU Billikens vs Michigan State. The Billikens guard their goal, L-R: Gerry Balassi, Joe Hennessey, Roger Rupp (goalie), Ed Oswald, Don Ceresia, Al Toczylowski, Dan Leahy, and Tom Klein. (22 November 1962) *[Photo by Father Luke]*

Page 49 bottom: NCAA Tournament, SLU Billikens vs Michigan State. SLU's Tom Klein heads a shot on Michigan State as Tom McDonnell (#13), Tom Mataya (#3) and Bill Vieth (on right) stand ready to follow-up. (22 November 1962) *[Photo by Father Luke]*

Page 50 top: NCAA Tournament, SLU Billikens vs Maryland in St. Louis,at Francis Field. The Billikens

celebrate another NCAA Championship. **First row** (L-R): Mrs. Balassi, Gerry Balassi, unknown, and unknown child. **Second row:** Tim Knox, unknown, Al Toczylowski, Roger Rupp, Don Ceresia, Coach Bob Guelker, Tom Mataya, Raymond Mann, Bill Vieth, Asst. Coach Tom Trost, and team manager Bill Tieman. **Third row:** Ed Oswald, Terry Knox, Dan Leahy, Fred Boyd, Jim Byron, Gerald Schwalbe, trainer Kim Tucci, James Rick, Joe Hennessey, Mike Moore, Bill Bayer, unknown, and Larry Cronin. (24 November 1962) *[Photo by Father Luke]*

1963

1963 BILLIKENS SOCCER CLUB SCHEDULE

DATE	OPPONENT	NICKNAME	PLACE	SLU	OPPONENT
21 Sept.	Air Force Academy	Falcons	Musial Field	4	0
25 Sept.	MacMurray College	Highlanders	Musial Field	3	0
28 Sept.	Ball State	Cardinals	Musial Field	12	0
4 Oct.	Notre Dame	Fighting Irish	Musial Field	8	1
12 Oct.	Wheaton College	Crusaders	Wheaton, IL	5	0
13 Oct.	Univ of Chicago	Maroons	Chicago, IL	16	0
19 Oct.	Washington Univ	Bears	St. Louis, MO	12	0
26 Oct.	Miami	Hurricanes	Miami, FL	6	0
2 Nov.	Illinois	Fighting Illini	Urbana-Champaign, IL	10	2
9 Nov.	Michigan State	Spartans	E. Lansing, MI	3	4
22 Nov.	Michigan State	Spartans	E. Lansing, MI	2	0
27 Nov.	Univ of San Francisco	Dons	St. Louis, MO	3	2
5 Dec.	Univ of Maryland	Terrapins	New Brunswick, NJ	7	3
7 Dec.	Navy	Middies	New Brunswick, NJ	3	0

1963 SLU Championship Soccer Team. Row 1 (L-R): Terry Knox, Tom Mataya, Carl Gentile, Pat McBride, Ray Mann, Tim Knox, Tom Layton, Gerry Schwalbe. **Row 2:** Dave Sirinek, Bob Ernst, Tom McDonnell, John Butler, Bill Vieth, Jack Gilsinn, Dan Leahy. **Row 3:** Coach Bob Guelker, Dave Behnen, Bill Bayer, Adrian Vanderzahm, Joe Hennessey, Kevin Kelly, Don Ceresia, Fred Boyd, Jim Bryon, Mike Moore, Roger Rupp, Manager Kim Tucci, Assistant Coach Al Toczylowski. *[By accident, this image was omitted from the 1964 Archive yearbook. Photo by Father Luke]*

The 1963 squad had a mountain to climb. Living up to the records and results set by previous teams was a daunting task. Nonetheless, the 1963 team was able to surpass previous triumphs and scored a school record of 94 goals, an average of 6.7 goals per game. Carl Gentile set another school record with 30 goals while Pat McBride had 17 assists, a school record that lasted until 1995. In spite of a late-season loss to Michigan State on November 9th, the team regrouped and proceeded to enact their revenge two weeks later, beating the Spartans 2-0. The season was capped by a 3-0 win over Navy, earning SLU their fourth national title. Joe Hennessey was named to the All-American team.

SIDELINE:
GUELKER'S RIVALS

During the Bob Guelker era, major rivals were Michigan State, the University of Maryland and the University of San Francisco. These teams had many accomplishments to be proud of. In particular, Michigan State only lost 10 games in the first 10 years of their soccer program's existence. The SLU Billikens were responsible for eight of those 10 Spartan losses!

MIDFIELD MEMORY:
A DAY I'LL NEVER FORGET

By Dan Leahy

It was Friday, November 22, 1963, just about noon. We were in East Lansing, Michigan, coming out of our hotel rooms at the Albert Pick hotel and boarding the bus which would take us to Michigan State's plush soccer stadium for our 2:00pm NCAA Midwest Regional showdown with the Spartans. We were on the road for this crucial match because, just two weeks earlier, we had lost 3-4 at East Lansing in our regular season finale. With what was clearly our strongest squad in my three varsity seasons as a soccer Billiken, we didn't expect to lose to anyone, anywhere, at any time. But in that final game of our 1963 regular schedule, we acted as if we were intimidated by the heavily foreign Michigan State squad, and in particular by their Jamaican star, Peyton Fuller. So there we were, back up north just outside of Detroit, many thoughts running through our minds as we got ready to begin this 'one-and-out' phase of the season.

We were getting close to departing for the stadium when one of the stragglers—John Butler, I believe—came running out of his room shouting to all of us on the bus that something unbelievable had just happened. The TV was still on in John's room, and the first reports of President Kennedy having been shot in Dallas were emerging via news bulletins. To all of us, and in particular to this 19-year-old junior, none of it made any sense. John Kennedy with his relative youth and ideals had become a symbol of change for the good in the political landscape of our country. We could relate to him—he was our hero and the leader of the free world! We all stood in complete bewilderment and confusion as reporters continued to broadcast more details. Coach Guelker then gently prodded us to reboard the bus, leaving us with the hope that this would have a positive ending.

I don't remember exactly when it was that we found out the worst, that in fact President Kennedy was dead. But as we quietly dressed for the game we all knew that we had lost our leader. As often strangely happens at times like these, we took the field and literally played our best. It was the most focused game of the season. It didn't make any difference who we were playing that afternoon, or that we had just been there two weeks earlier and suffered a critical defeat. Our main nemesis from that earlier match—Peyton Fuller from Jamaica—was disposed of in the first five minutes. My partner in the middle of our defense, Don Ceresia, and I caught Fuller just outside of the

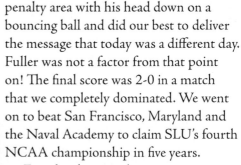

penalty area with his head down on a bouncing ball and did our best to deliver the message that today was a different day. Fuller was not a factor from that point on! The final score was 2-0 in a match that we completely dominated. We went on to beat San Francisco, Maryland and the Naval Academy to claim SLU's fourth NCAA championship in five years.

Exactly what it is that moves a group of young college athletes to go above and beyond their normal performance levels is always a matter of speculation. On this particular day, November 22, 1963, the tragic loss of our young American president created a single-minded focus that was directed that very afternoon at our unfortunate opponent, Michigan State. None of us who were there will ever forget it.

Page 53 top: SLU Billikens vs Ball State Cardinals at Fairgrounds Park in St. Louis. SLU's Kevin Kelly fires a shot past Ball State's players. (28 September 1963) *[Photo by Father Luke]*

Page 53 bottom: SLU Billikens vs Washington University. Bill Vieth dribbling down the sideline (19 Oct 1963) *[Photo by Father Luke]*

Page 54 bottom: SLU Billikens vs Washington University in St. Louis, MO. SLU's Carl Gentile watches his shot fly as Pat McBride (on right) looks on. (19 October 1963) *[Photo by Father Luke]*

Page 55 top: SLU Billikens vs Wash University. SLU's Joe Hennessey(#10) positions himself to block a shot, as Don Ceresia (on left) comes in to help. (19 October 1963) *[Photo by Father Luke]*

Page 55 bottom: SLU Billikens vs Washington University. SLU's Carl Gentile takes a shot on Washington University's goal. (19 October 1963) *[Photo by Father Luke]*

Page 56 & 57 top: SLU Billikens vs University of Miami.. SLU's Carl Gentile (#2) shoots with Pat McBride to his side and Tom Mataya looking on from the right. *[Photo by Father Luke]*

Page 56 bottom: SLU Billikens vs University of Miami Hurricanes, at Miami. Billiken players huddle with Coach Guelker on the sideline. (26 October 1963) *[Photo by Father Luke]*

Page 57 bottom: SLU Billikens vs University of Miami, at Miami. Billiken player, Terry Knox (#6), gains control of the ball from a Hurricane

defender. (26 October 1963) *[Photo by Father Luke]*

Page 58 top: SLU Billikens vs Olympians. All-American Joe Hennessey. (28 Dec 1963) *[Photo by Father Luke]*

1964

1964 BILLIKENS SOCCER CLUB SCHEDULE

DATE	OPPONENT	NICKNAME	PLACE	SLU	OPPONENT
26 Sept.	Air Force Academy	Falcons	Colorado Springs, CO	4	2
3 Oct.	Illinois	Fighting Illini	Urbana-Champaign, IL	16	0
7 Oct.	MacMurray College	Highlanders	Jacksonville, IL	8	1
10 Oct.	Navy Pier, UIC	Sailors	Chicago, IL	10	0
11 Oct.	Marquette	Golden Eagles	Milwaukee, WI	10	1
17 Oct.	Washington Univ	Bears	Magdalen Field	5	0
24 Oct.	Miami	Hurricanes	Magdalen Field	7	0
31 Oct.	Georgia Tech	Yellow Jackets	Fairgrounds Pk. #1	7	0
7 Nov.	Michigan State	Spartans	Fairgrounds Pk. #1	1	1
14 Nov.	Wheaton College	Crusaders	Fairgrounds Pk. #1	6	2
18 Nov.	Indiana Univ	Hoosiers	Fairgrounds Pk. #1	8	2
28 Nov.	San Jose State	Spartans	Fairgrounds Pk. #1	5	0
3 Dec.	Navy	Middies	Providence, RI	1	2

1964 SLU Soccer Team, Mid-Western Collegiate Soccer Conference Champions. Row 1(L-R): Kevin O'Connell, Tom Mataya, Tom Schoenbeck, Bob Ernst, Fred Boyd, Pat McBride, Jack Gilsinn, Carl Gentile, Don Brennan. **Row 2:** Dave Sirinek, Jim Murphy, Jack Kinealy, Bob Kerber, Ed Lipski, Dan Mannion, Bill Brown, Jerry Schwalbe, Timmy Knox. **Row 3:** Coach Bob Guelker, Gene Baker, Bob Garcia, Jay Moore, John Lacey, Don Ceresia, Dan Leahy, Terry Knox, Assistant Coach Bill Mueller and Manager Tom Daly. Missing from the photo: Tim McAuliffe. *[Photo by Father Luke]*

Not to be outdone by the previous year's squad, the 1964 Billikens averaged 6.8 goals per game including a 16-0 victory over the University of Illinois on October 3rd. Although they lost only one game that year, it was a heartbreaker to Navy in a rematch of the previous year's title game. Navy defeated SLU 2-1 in the national semifinal on December 3rd. This was the first year that SLU did not reach the national championship game. Carl Gentile led the team with 27 goals, and Don Ceresia and Pat McBride received All-American honors.

SIDELINE:
PRACTICE MAKES PERFECT!

Perhaps the reason there were no complaints from the players about not having a home field on campus was that there was no *practice* field on campus either.

Consistent with being a "commuter college," SLU players would travel to the University campus each day for class by car or bus. Then in the afternoon, they had to commute with other players from the West Pine (Frost) campus to a practice field located in the middle of Forest Park. This was especially challenging if the players did not have cars or had a class or lab at the Medical School further south on Grand Avenue.

Adjacent to the Forest Park practice field there were public restrooms, showers and locker rooms. Even so, most players commuted home after practice in their workout gear rather than showering and changing in the public restrooms.

One great memory evolved from practicing in Forest Park every day. All the players remember to this day how every practice ended with the team "running the hills" to get into and stay in top physical condition. Moan, whine, groan, and complain about the hills, they did, but pain aside, almost all believe it was one of the main reasons for Billiken success, especially in tight games. The Billikens simply were always in better shape than the competition.

Page 61 top: SLU Billikens vs Washington University. SLU's Carl Gentile looks to dribble around a Washington University defender, as Bob Ernst (left) and Jack Gilsinn (right) watch. (17 October 1964) *[Photo by Father Luke]*

Page 61 bottom: SLU Billikens vs Marquette University. SLU's Carl Gentile dances with the ball to juke a

defender. (11 October 1964) *[Photo by Father Luke]*

Page 62: SLU Billikens vs Washington University. Surrounded by opponents, SLU All-American, Pat McBride, takes a shot (17 October 1964) *[Photo by Father Luke]*

Page 63 top right: SLU Billikens vs Washington University. SLU's Jack Kinealy watches his shot,

flanked by Jay Moore (on left). (17 October 1964) *[Photo by Father Luke]*

Page 63 middle right: SLU Billikens vs Wheaton. SLU's Dan Leahy goes for a head ball as Jim Murphy (behind the play) stands ready to help. Gene Baker and goalie Fred Boyd (on the right) look on. (14 Nov 1964) *[Photo by Father Luke]*

Page 63 bottom right: SLU Billikens vs Wheaton in St. Louis. The Billikens' defense stands ready for Wheaton strike. L-R: Jerry Schwalbe, Don Brennan (goalie), Don Ceresia, Dan Leahy, Bob Ernst, and Ed Lipski (14 November 1964) *[Photo by Father Luke]*

Page 64: SLU Billikens vs Miami University. SLU's Pat McBride fires a shot past a Miami defender. SLU

teammates (L-R) Terry Knox, Tim Knox, and Jack Kinealy watch the action. (24 October 1964) *[Photo by Father Luke]*

Page 66: SLU Billikens vs Michigan State. SLU's Dan Leahy heads the ball over a Spartan player. (07 November 1964) *[Photo by Father Luke]*

1965

1965 BILLIKENS SOCCER CLUB SCHEDULE

DATE	OPPONENT	NICKNAME	PLACE	SLU	OPPONENT
25 Sept.	Illinois	Fighting Illini	Urbana-Champaign, IL	6	0
2 Oct.	Wheaton College	Crusaders	Wheaton, IL	1	0
3 Oct.	Northwestern	Wildcats	Chicago, IL	4	0
9 Oct.	Notre Dame	Fighting Irish	South Bend, IN	10	0
16 Oct.	Air Force Academy	Falcons	Musial Field	4	0
23 Oct.	Miami	Hurricanes	Miami, FL	6	2
30 Oct.	Alumni		Musial Field	6	1
6 Nov.	Michigan State	Spartans	E. Lansing, MI	3	2
10 Nov.	MacMurray College	Highlanders	Fairgrounds Pk. #1	5	1
13 Nov.	Marquette	Warriors	Musial Field	10	0
20 Nov.	Ohio	Bobcats	Fairgrounds Pk. #1	2	1
27 Nov.	Univ of San Francisco	Dons	San Francisco, CA	5	2
2 Dec.	Navy	Middies	Fairgrounds Pk. #1	3	1
4 Dec.	Michigan State	Spartans	Francis Field	1	0

1965 SLU Championship Soccer Team. Players are identified as follows, **Row 1** (L-R): Sal Grasso, Steve Rick, Jay Moore, Pat McBride, Jack Kinnealy, Wally Werner, Carl Gentile, Bob Kerber. **Row 2:** Trainer Tom Daily, Dave Schlitt, Bob Miramonti, Tom Stahl, Vince Drake, Bob Garcia, Jim Murphy, Ron Johnson, Gene Baker, Manager Gary Baumstark. **Row 3:** Coach Bob Guelker, Tony Tocco, Tim McAuliffe, Don Brennan, Frank Fletcher, Jack Gilsinn, Bob Veith, Tom Hennessy, Joe Westhus, Bob Fitzgerald.

When the 1965 season began, Coach Guelker had only three regular starters returning from the previous year. A total of 17 players with limited or no experience filled out the rest of the roster. With the success of previous teams, it seemed impossible to achieve the one feat that eluded the program—a perfect season. Although this was supposed to be a rebuilding year for the program, the Billikens charged out of the gate and never looked back. The team was 13-0 when entering the championship match against a Michigan State team that featured eight native St. Louis players. The Billikens prevailed in a tightly contested, defensive game winning 1-0, thus achieving a truly perfect season. Jack Kinealy led the team in scoring with 23 goals, and Carl Gentile and Pat McBride were named All-Americans. While Gentile and McBride received most of the accolades in 1965 for their goal scoring and play making abilities, the other key piece of that year's arsenal was center-half Jack Gilsinn. His take-no-prisoners attitude set the standard for the Billikens' hard-to-penetrate defense that year. At the conclusion of the 1965 season, the NCAA had conducted seven NCAA Tournaments in soccer. SLU had won five of the titles and made it to the "final four" the other two years.

SIDELINE:
THE ARCH

In 1965, as the Billiken soccer program was in pursuit of its fifth national championship in seven years, the iconic Gateway Arch was nearing completion on the St. Louis Riverfront. Originally designed in 1947 as part of a concept competition for the Jefferson National Expansion Memorial project, the actual start of construction was in February 1963. As the Arch was nearing its completion in October 1965, a great deal of local and national attention was directed to the complex placement of the final piece at the very top of the Arch.

Once completed, the Arch quickly became one of the most popular attractions in America. It symbolized the westward expansion of our great country, just as the Billiken soccer dynasty became instantly recognized as the benchmark, and conduit, of American collegiate soccer expansion. By the end of the 1965 campaign, Coach Bob Guelker and his Billikens had completed another successful NCAA Championship journey, giving Coach Guelker his final championship at SLU.

MIDFIELD MEMORY:

RELOADING, NOT REBUILDING

By Jim Murphy

It's the second Tuesday in August 1965. The SLU men's soccer team is having its first tryout session for the upcoming season. Our returning starters are worried.

They have good reason to worry. Gone from last year's team are nine key contributors:

1. Three of the four starting defensive backfield, including (a) a two-time MVP of the NCAA tournament, first team All-American, and one of last year's co-captains; and (b) a three-year starter, all Midwest Conference player, and the other co-captain from last year's team;
2. The top two goalies from last year's team;
3. Three of the five starters from last year's high-scoring forward line; and
4. One of the starting mid-fielders from last year's NCAA semi-finalist team.

Still the team is not without its strengths. The team is returning its two Olympians and All-Americans, Pat McBride and Carl Gentile, along with two-year starter, rugged defender Jack Gilsinn. Some of the players who are moving up to starter status had seen significant playing time last year; others had seen limited action. A few will be playing as Billikens for the first time. The prevailing feeling among the new starters is, "Although the team might have lost some great players, 1965 is now our time. Let's go prove we deserve to be here."

The finals of the 1965 NCAA tournament will be held in St. Louis in December. But the key game the Billikens play takes place three weeks before. It's the last game of the regular conference season. The game is an away game against undefeated archrival Michigan State. After flying "White Cloud" to the airport in East Lansing on Friday afternoon, the team is somber on its bus ride to the on-campus, student-run hotel. Upon check-in, team captains McBride and Gentile hold a team meeting in their hotel room. No coaches are invited. After everyone squeezes

into the hotel room, Gentile opens the curtains covering the two large windows in the room and uses a bar of soap to sketch an outline of a soccer field. For the next 45 minutes, McBride and Gentile draw out and go over the defensive and offensive responsibilities of each position. They review the Spartans' lineup by position and assign certain Bills to shadow certain opponents "wherever they go, even if it's to the men's room!"

On Saturday, the Bills are quiet yet confident as they go to the field. The game is a typical SLU versus Michigan State game, hard fought and close. Deep into the second half, Carl Gentile streaks through the middle of the Spartans' defense. In desperation, the MSU center-back attempts a football tackle to prevent a breakaway. As Carl shakes off his tackler, the Spartan yanks Gentile's shoe part way off his foot. Gentile dashes down the last few yards to the penalty area and scores with his shoe half off. The goal takes the starch out of the Spartans and the Bills control the rest of the game, dominating the midfield play.

The first Saturday in December 1965 comes in as a sunny yet brisk St. Louis day. Francis Field, the home of Washington University, welcomes over 10,000 people into its stands for the NCAA finals. For most of the Billikens, this is the largest crowd they have ever played.

The opening ceremony calls for the two starting elevens to stand along the sideline as the national anthem is played. It's hard for the Billikens to stand still. Most are bouncing up and down, either to keep loose or to deal with the extra adrenaline flowing through their bodies. They look across the field at the Spartans' lineup. Many glare at the five St. Louisans on the Michigan State team. These five are the first group of athletes from the St. Louis area to be recruited en masse to a major college on soccer scholarships. These were the highly touted, big-name high school players many of the Billikens played with or against in high school, CYC or club ball. Although they may have been friends or teammates back then, the rivalry turns to hostility upon seeing these St. Louisans dressed in

Spartan green and white rather than Billiken blue and white. As the national anthem ends, most vow, "Today all of St. Louis will learn who the real college soccer champions are!"

The game is a bruising, take-no-prisoners game. Although each team is noted for its high scoring offense, each team's defense is stout, rugged and refuses to be beaten. In the second half, the Spartans take the physical play a step too far, viciously fouling Carl Gentile in the penalty area. With the demeanor of a steely-eyed gunslinger, he makes the penalty kick, and the winning goal. The Bills are national champions for the fifth time in seven years, becoming the only undefeated, untied Billiken team in the school's history.

SIDELINE:

NO SOCCER SCHOLARSHIPS, BUT BASEBALL MONEY HELPS

Coach Guelker and SLU baseball coach Roy Lee cooperated with each other and provided "baseball scholarships" to a few SLU players who played both varsity baseball and soccer. Of particular note is the 1965 SLU baseball team. It is the only SLU baseball team to ever advance to play in the NCAA College World Series, finishing third in the country. Four stars on that 1965 baseball team, Carl Gentile, Dan Leahy, Jim Murphy and Tony Tocco, also were members of the 1964 and 1965 SLU soccer teams.

Page 69 top: SLU Billikens vs Northwestern University in Chicago. SLU's Jack Kinealy cuts the ball back, as Jay Moore runs alongside and Jim Murphy (on far left) trails behind. (3 October 1965) *[Photo by Father Luke]*

Page 69 bottom: SLU Billikens vs Air Force Academy. SLU's Pat McBride crosses the ball as Jim Murphy (on left) and Gene Baker (on right in background) track with the play. (16 October 1965) *[Photo by Father Luke]*

Page 70: SLU Billikens vs University of Illinois. SLU's Tim McAuliffe (#9) battles for ball control as Pat McBride (#2) looks on. The St. Louis Arch construction, in the background, nears completion. (25 September 1965) *[Photo by Father Luke]*

Page 73 top: SLU Billikens vs Michigan State. SLU All-American Wally Werner weaves the ball around a Michigan State defender. (6 November 1965) *[Photo by Father Luke]*

Page 73 bottom: SLU Billikens vs Michigan State. SLU's Wally Werner moves the ball forward, backed-up by Jim Murphy (left) and Pat McBride (right). (6 November 1965) *[Photo by Father Luke]*

Page 74 top: SLU Billikens vs Ohio University in the NCAA Quarter Final. SLU's Jack Kinnealy takes a shot on goal. (20 November 1965) *[Photo by Father Luke]*

Page 74 bottom: NCAA Tournament Final. SLU Billikens vs Michigan State at Washington University in St. Louis, MO. SLU's Pat McBride, Carl Gentile, and Jack Gilsinn gather at midfield for the pre-game coin toss. (04 December 1965) *[Photo by Father Luke]*

Page 75 top: SLU Billikens vs Ohio University in the NCAA Quarter Final. SLU All-American Jack Kinealy races to the ball. (20 November 1965) *[Photo by Father Luke]*

Page 75 bottom: SLU Billikens vs Michigan State. SLU's Carl Gentile heads the ball as his Billiken teammates look on, L-R: Joe Westhus, Jack Gilsinn, Don Brennan (goalie), Tim McAuliffe, Jim Murphy and Gene Baker (04 December 1965) *[Photo by Father Luke]*

Page 76 top: SLU Billikens vs Michigan State. SLU's Wally Werner keeps the ball from Spartan players as Jim Murphy "supports" the play. (04 December 1965) *[Photo by Father Luke]*

Page 76 bottom: Don Brennan, Billiken goalie, makes a save against the Michigan State Spartans in the Final game of the NCAA Playoffs. (4 December 1965) *[Photo by T. Mike Fletcher]*

Page 77 top: SLU Billikens vs Michigan State in St. Louis, MO. SLU's Jack Gilsinn jumps for the ball as Gene Baker watches from behind. (04 December 1965) *[Photo by Father Luke]*

Page 78: Salute to 1965, National Champs, The University News (10 December, 1965)

1 For The Money

DAVE SCHLITT ATTEMPTS a goal against Northwestern, a game which was the third of the Bills' opening shutouts, 4-0.

2 For The Show

AGAINST AIR FORCE, another 4-0 victim of St. Louis, outside left forward Jay Moore pedals the ball toward the Falcons' goal. These early successes, helped gain the NCAA bid for the Bills.

3 To Get Ready

IN A MATCH FOR A BERTH IN THE NCAA FINALS, the San Francisco goalie watches Pat McBride bore in and pass off. The Bills beat Ohio U. 2-1 in an earlier play off game. The Dons dropped a 5-2 decision.

Salute To 1965

National Champs

And 4 To Go

CAPPING THE SEASON was Carl Gentile's penalty kick against Michigan State. Gentile here fakes and weaves to get an unblocked kick.

For 5th NCAA Title

THE SPARTAN GOALIE OUT OF POSITION, Gentile's kick goes in and gives the Billikens their fifth National Collegiate Athletic Association Soccer Championship.

1966

1966 BILLIKENS SOCCER CLUB SCHEDULE

DATE	OPPONENT	NICKNAME	PLACE	SLU	OPPONENT
24 Sept.	Air Force Academy	Falcons	Colorado Springs, CO	2	0
28 Sept.	Quincy	Hawks	Quincy, IL	1	2
30 Sept.	Indiana Univ	Hoosiers	Bloomington, IN	2	2
2 Oct.	Rockhurst	Hawks	Kansas City, MO	0	1
8 Oct.	British Columbia	Thunderbirds	Musial Field	1	0
9 Oct.	Kutis		Musial Field	1	2
15 Oct.	MacMurray College	Highlanders	Jacksonville, IL	5	0
22 Oct.	Miami	Hurricanes	Musial Field	9	0
23 Oct.	Northwestern	Wildcats	Musial Field	6	0
29 Oct.	Alumni		Musial Field	0	0
5 Nov.	Michigan State	Spartans	Musial Field	1	1
12 Nov.	Illinois	Fighting Illini	Urbana-Champaign, IL	4	1
20 Nov.	Colorado College	Tigers	Colorado Springs, CO	5	1
26 Nov.	Univ of San Francisco	Dons	San Francisco, CA	1	2

1966 SLU Soccer Team. Row 1 (L-R): Ron Johnson, Tom Bokern, Jim Conley, Larry Warren, Don Brennan, Tony Tocco, Tom Walsh, Wally Werner. **Row 2:** Steve Rick, Brad Melchior, Tom Rich, Bob Kerber, Jack Kinealy, Jay Moore, Tom Stahl, Joe Westhus. **Row 3:** Coach Bob Guelker, Gary Baumstark, Tim McAuliffe, Dave Schlitt, Bob Garcia, Jerry Diekemper, Jim Leeker, Jim Puzniak, Jim Murphy. Missing from the photo are Frank Fletcher, Bob Miramonti, and Vince Drake.

A significant development occurred off the playing field for SLU soccer in 1966. For the first time SLU untied its financial purse strings and allowed Coach Guelker to offer significant soccer scholarships to incoming recruits. The SLU administration realized this step was necessary for SLU to continue their level of excellence in soccer, as other college teams were now heavily recruiting local St. Louis players. The scholarships enabled Coach Guelker to secure a deep and talented class that would form the backbone of the SLU soccer team from

1967 to 1969. Remember, freshmen were not then eligible to play under existing NCAA rules. Members of the 1966 recruiting class included Gary Rensing, Steve Frank, John Pisani, Chuck Zoeller, Gene Geimer, and Bill McDermott. The irony of this scholarship decision by SLU was that Bob Guelker never had the opportunity to coach that class. Before that group was eligible to play on the field as sophomores, Coach Guelker had departed SLU to take a full-time coaching position at Southern Illinois University-Edwardsville (SIUE).

The last year of Coach Guelker's employment at SLU was the 1966 season. Over the previous eight seasons, Guelker's teams won 88 games while losing only six. While giving up less than one goal per game during the 1966 campaign, the Billikens lost a defensive struggle to the University of San Francisco in the second round of the NCAA Tournament by a score of 2-1. Jack Kinealy again led the team in scoring, this time with 11 goals, and took home All-American honors along with Steve Rick.

SIDELINE:

BOB GUELKER

The story of the Billikens' soccer dynasty does not start in 1959. Rather, it begins with the hiring of Bob Stewart as SLU's Athletic Director in 1958. Upon his arrival, Stewart was bombarded with calls, letters, and messages urging him to add soccer as a sport at SLU. When Bob Guelker, then the Executive Secretary of the Catholic Youth Council heard that soccer might be considered, he dropped by Stewart's office to add his encouragement. As Bob Guelker used to tell it, "I stopped by to give him encouragement and left with a job."

Bob Guelker became the first Billiken soccer coach, serving from 1958 until 1966. As a part-time employee of SLU, Coach Guelker also retained his full-time position with the CYC. Prior to joining the CYC, he had been employed as the Physical Education Director at the St. Louis Preparatory Seminary where he also served for many years as the soccer coach.

Athletic Director Stewart and Coach Guelker formed a club team in 1958 to help determine whether or not they should add soccer as a varsity sport. Rumor has it that when Guelker and Stewart presented a proposed $2,000 budget to SLU President Father Paul Reinert, S.J. for the start-up year of the soccer program, Father Reinert held true to another fine Jesuit tradition: he approved a reduced budget amount of $200. To stay within the budget, Coach Guelker agreed to serve as an unpaid, non-faculty coach for the first year. He remained a non-faculty coach at SLU throughout his years of service.

The 1958 club team achieved a record of 4-0-1, passing the test, and SLU made the decision to field its first varsity soccer team in 1959. That same year, the NCAA officially sanctioned soccer as a varsity sport for the first time. In its first varsity season, with players exclusively born and raised in St. Louis, the Billikens brought home the national championship with a thrilling 5-2 victory over the University of Bridgeport in Storrs, CT.

Coach Guelker's Billiken teams compiled a 95-10-5 record in his eight years as soccer coach. The teams won five NCAA championships: 1959, 1960, 1962, 1963 and 1965. SLU made it to the semi-finals in 1964, and the quarterfinals in 1966. The 1962 and the 1965 teams were undefeated, and the 1965 team was undefeated and untied.

In 1967 Coach Guelker left SLU to start up the new Men's Soccer Program at Southern Illinois University-Edwardsville (SIUE). While at SIUE, Coach Guelker would win the NCAA Division II Championship in 1972, and his sixth and final NCAA Division I Championship in 1979. Coach Guelker grew to be an ambassador for both SLU and college soccer. He served on the board of the U.S. Soccer Federation. In 1963 he coached the U.S. Olympic team as well as the Pan-American team. In 1964 Coach Guelker coached the U.S. Junior Olympic team. He was elected to the National Soccer Hall of Fame in 1980. Bob Guelker passed away on February 22, 1986 at the age of 62.

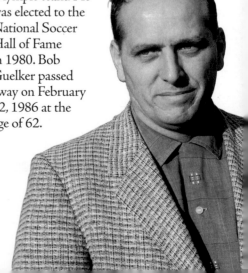

Page 81 top: SLU Billikens vs Kutis at Musial Field in St. Louis. SLU players, L-R: Wally Werner (#6), Tom Bokern, Dave Schlitt (#16), Jay Moore, Jim Leeker (#8). (9 October 1966) *[Photo by Father Luke]*

Page 81 bottom: SLU Billikens vs Kutis. Tom Bokern heads the ball as Jack Kinealy looks on. (9 October 1966) *[Photo by Father Luke]*

Page 82: SLU Billikens vs Kutis at Musial Field in St. Louis. SLU's Jack Kinealy controls the ball, trailed by teammate Ron Johnson. (9 October 1966) *[Photo by Father Luke]*

Page 83 top: SLU Billikens vs Kutis at Musial Field in St. Louis. Onlooking players L-R: Jim Leeker, Joe Westhus, Brad Melchoir, Don Brennan (goalie), and Tom Rich. (9 October 1966) *[Photo by Father Luke]*

Page 83 bottom: SLU Billikens vs Northwestern University. SLU All-American, Steve Rick, shoots a penalty kick as Tom Rich and Jim Murphy look on. (23 October 1966) *[Photo by Faher Luke]*

Page 84 & 85 top: SLU Billikens vs Kutis at Musial Field in St. Louis. Kutis player Steve Auberry (#11) takes a shot on SLU. Players L-R: Jim Leeker, Tom Bokern, Jack Kinealy, Don Brennan (goalie), Steve Rick, Dave Schlitt, and Brad Melchior (9 October 1966) *[Photo by Father Luke]*

Page 84 bottom: SLU Billikens vs Northwestern University. SLU's Jim Leeker (left) and Jack Kinealy await a rebound from Jay Moore's head ball on goal. (23 October 1966) *[Photo by Father Luke]*

Page 86: Program for the 1966 NCAA Soccer Regional Elimination Game, SLU vs Colorado College. (20 November 1966) *[Hosted and published by Colorado College, Colorado Springs. Program courtesy of Jim Leeker.]*

NCAA SOCCER

Colorado College
vs.
St. Louis University

Regional Elimination Game

November 20, 1966   *Colorado Springs, Colorado*

1967

1967 BILLIKENS SOCCER CLUB SCHEDULE

DATE	OPPONENT	NICKNAME	PLACE	SLU	OPPONENT
16 Sept.	Alumni		Magdalen Field	0	4
23 Sept.	Air Force Academy	Falcons	Magdalen Field	4	1
4 Oct.	SIU Carbondale	Salukis	Carbondale, IL	4	5
11 Oct.	South Florida	Bulls	Magdalen Field	1	0
14 Oct.	Rockhurst	Hawks	Magdalen Field	3	1
21 Oct.	Quincy	Hawks	Magdalen Field	1	0
30 Oct.	Michigan State	Spartans	E. Lansing, MI	3	3
4 Nov.	Indiana Univ	Hoosiers	Magdalen Field	4	0
11 Nov.	South Florida	Bulls	Tampa, FL	0	1
18 Nov.	Colorado College	Tigers	Colorado	6	1
25 Nov.	San Jose State	Spartans	San Jose, CA	4	3
30 Nov.	Navy	Middies	Francis Field	1	0
2 Dec.	Michigan State	Spartans	Francis Field	0	0

1967 SLU National Co-Championship Soccer Team.
Row 1 (L-R): Tim Brassil, John Pisani, Chuck Zoeller, Wally Werner, Tom Bokern, Bill McDermott, George Merubia, Rudy Roeslein. **Row 2:** Gene Geimer, Mike Poston, Stan Rozanski, Steve Frank, Tom Rich, Bob Hederman, Brad Melchior, Dave Schlitt. **Row 3:** Manager Mike Griffin, Gary Rensing, Jack Galmiche, Irv Mueller, Bill Donley, Wayne Fischer, Larry Warren, Jim Conley, Assistant Coach Val Pelizzaro and Coach Harry Keough. *[Photo by Father Luke]*

SLU entered the 1967 season under new head coach, Harry Keough. The team only tallied 31 goals in 13 games on its way to an 8-3-2 record and gave up a record 19 goals. However, they won when it was necessary and eventually fought their way to the NCAA final. There, they faced a now very familiar opponent, Michigan State. The match took place during a rainstorm that flooded the field, which was already saturated from several days of rain, and earned the nickname "Mud Game." The field conditions were so bad the game was called in the 42nd minute. At that point, the two teams had played to a scoreless tie. The NCAA named SLU and Michigan State co-champions, giving the Billikens their sixth national title and the Spartans their first. John Pisani led the team with six goals and Wally Werner took home All-American honors.

SIDELINE:

HARRY KEOUGH

In 1967, Harry Keough became the second coach in the history of the soccer program at SLU. At the time of his arrival as coach, Keough was already a well-known soccer personality in the St. Louis community, having played on three World Cup teams (1950, 1954 and 1958), served as captain of the U. S. Men's Olympic team (1952 and 1956), and enjoyed a long, illustrious career with the St. Louis Kutis soccer team. Harry would go on to coach the Billikens for 16 seasons. During his tenure, his teams compiled a record of 213-50-22, won five national championships, and missed the NCAA tournament only once. Keough retired as SLU head coach in 1982.

Harry Joseph Keough was born on November 15, 1927 in St. Louis. In 1945, he joined the St. Louis Schumachers soccer club, but left in 1946 to join the U.S. Navy. While stationed in California, he continued to play soccer, returning to St. Louis in the late 1940s. While later playing in the St. Louis Municipal League, he was chosen for the U.S. National team as it attempted to qualify for the 1950 World Cup. Keough achieved great success with the national team as a fullback and, along with four other St. Louis players, pulled off what is considered to be the greatest upset in World Cup history, a 1-0 defeat of heavily favored England. This game is the subject of the 2005 movie, *The Miracle Match* (a.k.a. *The Game of Their Lives*).

Keough was inducted into the National Soccer Hall of Fame in 1976 and into the National Soccer Club Coaches Association of America in 1996. In 2004, the Keough Award was established as an annual award given to the top male and female soccer players from the St. Louis area.

When Harry joined the Billikens as their coach, it was in a part-time capacity, as he continued his full-time employment with the U.S. Postal Service. Harry was, and still is, known for his love of telling stories, a result of the great memory he inherited from his father, Paddy Keough. Harry's son Ty was an exceptionally talented player who played for Harry from 1975 to 1978. Ty also followed in his father's footsteps in serving as a member of the U.S. National Team as well as becoming a college soccer head coach. In addition to Ty, Harry and his wife, Alma, have two daughters.

SIDELINE:
VAL PELIZZARO

From 1967 through 1996, Val Pelizzaro served as the assistant coach for SLU's men's soccer team. Pelizzaro came on board in 1967 with his good friend, Harry Keough, and remained in that capacity when Joe Clarke took over the head coaching reins from Keough. Pelizzaro worked at SLU with Keough for 14 years and with Clarke for 17 years. One of his primary roles as the assistant coach was to serve as the team's fitness trainer. Running, jumping and crawling up the Forest Park practice fields hill is indelibly etched in the memory of each of the SLU players Pelizzaro helped tutor.

He always led by example, running the hill and playing small games with the players

He was always positive and encouraging in his motivational style. Everyone knows Pelizzaro was a key contributor to the wonderful Kutis teams of the 1950s and early 1960s. Since he seldom talked about his other athletic exploits, few are aware that Pelizzaro won 12 varsity letters at St. Mary's High School in St. Louis while participating in four sports - soccer, baseball, track and football. He also briefly attended Arizona State on a football scholarship as a running back. He then left college after one year to join the U.S. Army during the Korean War.

While one would think 30 years of college coaching would be enough for most, not for Pelizzaro. In 1997 he relocated to Washington University in St. Louis with Joe Clarke to continue to serve as Joe's assistant in coaching the men's soccer team. In his spare time, he has helped coach the soccer

team at Visitation Academy since 1996.

When in the late fall of 2009 Pelizzaro finally retired from helping coach the Washington University men's team, that University hosted a post-game ceremony and reception honoring his service. A large number of former SLU and Washington University players showed up for the evening's festivities. The attendance was a tangible demonstration of the affection and respect that former players universally held for Pelizzaro. More than a few players, however, remarked that they were attending simply because they could not believe that he was finally going to hand in his college coaching boots after 40 plus years. Pelizzaro and his wife, Laura, have six children. Four of their sons—Tom, Matt, Tony and Mike— played on SLU soccer teams coached by their father.

Page 89 top: SLU Billikens vs. South Florida. Jack Galmiche heads shot on goal. (11 November 1967)

Page 89 bottom: SLU Billikens vs SIU. SLU's Wally Werner shoots, flanked by Steve Frank (on left) and Brad Melchior (on right). (4 October 1967) *[Photo by Father Luke]*

Page 90: SLU Billikens Men's Soccer. Coach Harry Keough poses with John Pisani, Jack Galmiche and Tom Rich (18 September 1968) *[Photo by Father Luke]*

Page 91 top: SLU Coach Val Pelizzaro (on left) oversees a Billikens practice. Players, L-R: Doug De Sa Queen, Tim Logush, Jim Draude and Mike Seerey. (7 December 1971) *[Photo by Globe-Democrat photographer Dick Weddle]*

Page 92 top: SLU Billikens vs SIU in Carbondale, IL. SLU's Chuck Zoeller fires a shot, as teammates (L-R) John Pisani, Gary Rensing and Steve Frank look on. (4 October 1967) *[Photo by Father Luke]*

Page 92 & 93 bottom: SLU Billikens vs Rockhurst Hawks at Magdalen Field in St. Louis. SLU's Wally Werner (on right) passes the ball as (L-R) Brad Melchior and Chuck Zoeller (#17) stand ready to join the action. (14 October 1967) *[Photo by Father Luke]*

Page 93 top: SLU Billikens vs Rockhurst. SLU's Wally Werner slides for the ball as (L-R) Gene Geiner (#10), Brad Melchior, and Bill McDermott support the play. (14 October 1967) *[Photo by Father Luke]*

Page 94: SLU Billikens vs Rockhurst Hawks at Magdalen Field in St. Louis. SLU's Chuck Zoeller moves the ball, supported by (L-R) Bill McDermott, Dave Schlitt, Gene Geimer and Gary Rensing. (14 October 1967) *[Photo by Father Luke]*

Page 95: SLU Billikens vs Rockhurst Hawks at Magdalen Field in St. Louis. SLU's Chuck Zoeller (#17) unloads a shot between two Rockhurst defenders as (L-R) Tom Bokern and John Pisani look on. (14 October 1967) *[Photo by Father Luke]*

Page 96: 1967 Billiken Soccer: Follow The Bills As They Seek Their NCAA Title, The University News, (22 September 1967)

TOM BOKERN

WALLY WERNER

1967
Billiken
SOCCER

HOME GAMES			AWAY GAMES		
Sept. 16	Alumni	2:00 p.m.	Oct. 4	So. Illinois	4:00 p.m.
Sept. 23	Air Force	2:00 p.m.	Oct. 28	Michigan State	2:00 p.m.
Sept. 30	South Florida	2:00 p.m.	Nov. 11	South Florida	2:00 p.m.
Oct. 14	Rock Hurst	2:00 p.m.			
Oct. 21	Quincy	2:00 p.m.			
Nov. 4	Indiana	2:00 p.m.			

FOLLOW THE BILLS AS THEY SEEK THEIR NCAA TITLE

ADULTS $1.00   STUDENTS 50ᶜ

Round-Trip Bus Leaves Gym at 1:15 — Fare 50ᶜ

1968

1968 BILLIKENS SOCCER CLUB SCHEDULE

DATE	OPPONENT	NICKNAME	PLACE	SLU	OPPONENT
9 Sept.	Air Force Academy	Falcons	Colorado Springs, CO	1	0
22 Sept.	Colorado College	Tigers	Colorado Springs, CO	4	0
29 Sept.	Alumni		Musial Field	4	0
5 Oct.	South Florida	Bulls	Musial Field	3	1
13 Oct.	Rockhurst	Hawks	Kansas City, MO	3	1
15 Oct.	SIU Carbondale	Salukis	Musial Field	6	0
19 Oct.	Quincy	Hawks	Quincy, IL	2	1
26 Oct.	Michigan State	Spartans	Musial Field	0	0
2 Nov.	Indiana Univ	Hoosiers	Bloomington, IN	5	0
10 Nov.	Washington Univ	Bears	Francis Field	6	0
16 Nov.	West Virginia	Mountaineers	Musial Field	3	2
22 Nov.	Univ of Maryland	Terrapins	College Park, MD	1	3

1968 SLU Soccer Team. Row 1: Joe Leeker, Erminio DiMambro, Al Trost, Jim Draude, Gene Geimer, Jim Leeker, Chuck Zoeller, John Pisani. **Row 2:** Harry Amann, Jim Evans, Rudy Roeslein, Bill McDermott, Tim Flynn, Stan Rozanski, Tom Rich, Steve Frank, Ed Neusel. **Row 3:** Assistant Coach Val Pelizzaro, Jack Galmiche, Jim Niehoff, Tim O'Toole, Don Copple, Larry Warren, Bill Donley, Wayne Fischer, Gary Rensing, Head Coach Harry Keough. (Missing from the photo: Tom Bokern). *[Photo by Father Luke]*

The 1968 squad featured a much improved defense, a specialty of Keough's, giving up only eight goals the entire season. The team again made it to the NCAA finals, squaring off against familiar opponent, Maryland. Maryland gave SLU their only loss of the season on November 22nd, defeating them 3-1. John Pisani led the team in scoring with eight goals, and Steve Frank was named an All-American. In addition, former Billikens Jack Kinealy and Jay Moore were named to that year's Olympic squad.

SIDELINE:

GOALIES! WHO WOULD HAVE THOUGHT?

The stereotypical soccer goalie is brave but not necessarily noted as being the most intelligent player on the team. The common thinking is that a goalie's diminished capacity is not due to the fact they were born that way, but instead is the product of fearlessly diving for the ball at the feet of opposing players. As a result most goalies have been kicked in the head more than a few times, and we all know how that usually affects mental capacity. But the SLU goalies during SLU's championship years were able to break this stereotype.

Don Brennan was a goalie on the Billiken teams from 1964 to 1966. After his playing days at SLU were over, Don continued to pursue graduate work, eventually completing his Ph.D. at the University of Oklahoma. After a brief Air Force career, Don returned home to St. Louis as well as Saint Louis University, joining the Department of Communication Disorders as an Associate Instructor. Within a few years, he became chairman of that department. Another few years later, he was asked to become Dean of the Graduate School. Three years ago, he was asked to accept additional responsibilities and the title of Dean of the College of Arts & Science. Today Don remains Dean of the two schools as well as Associate Provost for Research. Don was the second person Father Biondi hired when he became President of Saint Louis University. Don's close working relationship with Father Biondi and his fierce loyalty to the University are traits you would expect from someone who put such a high value on hard work and teamwork during his days on the playing field.

Tony Tocco was a goalie on the Billikens teams from 1965 to 1966. Tony never really put his playing days behind him. He simply changed his location from the playing field to the coach's box. After completing his undergraduate studies at SLU in 1967, Tony earned both his masters degree and his Ph.D. in Accounting from SLU. Tocco has since spent the last 39 years as a full-time professor and head of the accounting department at Rockhurst University in Kansas City. In some circles, however, Tony is better known for his accomplishments as the head coach of the Rockhurst Hawks soccer team over that same time frame. His 574 career victories rank first among active intercollegiate coaches and third on the all-time coaching list. His Rockhurst Hawks were a perennial power in the NAIA from 1973 to 1997. Tocco, who was inducted into the NAIA Hall of Fame in 2007, was named the NAIA National Coach of the Year three times (1974, 1976 and 1986). Since joining the NCAA in 1998, the Hawks

have posted a 118-48-21 record. He was named National Coach of the Year in 1986 by the NSCAA.

Chuck Zorumski played as a goalkeeper for the SLU teams from 1972 to 1974. He was a member of the U.S. Olympic and National teams from 1973 to 1975. After graduating from SLU in 1974, Chuck earned his doctoral degree in Psychiatry from SLU in 1978. His academic achievements are too numerous to cover. Chuck is now the Chairman of the Department of Psychiatry at the School of Medicine at Washington University in St. Louis. Chuck is a renowned expert on depression and its treatment.

Well done, Don, Tony and Chuck.

NCAA Champs 6 of Last 9 Years

1968
BILLIKEN
SOCCER

Defending NCAA Co-Champions

Page 99 top: SLU Billikens vs Michigan State at Musial Field in St. Louis, MO. Jack Galmiche moves in on goal. (26 October 1968) *[Photo by Father Luke]*

Page 99 bottom: SLU Billikens Men's Soccer. SLU's Al Trost shoots the ball past Michigan State defenders. (1968) *[Excerpted from 1969 Archive yearbook, page 213. Photographer unknown.]*

Page 100 bottom: SLU Billikens Men's soccer. Jim Leeker heads a ball on goal as Al Trost (center) stands by to follow up. Jack Galmiche moves in

from the left to help out. (1968) *[Photographer unknown; photo courtesy of Jim Leeker]*

Page 101 top: SLU Billikens vs SIU Carbondale at Musial Field in St. Louis. SLU's Chuck Zoeller creates a cloud of dust as he shoots a penalty kick. (15 October 1968) *[Excerpted from 1969 Archive yearbook, page 213. Photographer unknown.]*

Page 101 bottom: SLU Billikens vs SLU Alumni. SLU's Al Trost makes a cut to dribble around defenders, as Steve Frank (far right) looks on. (26 October 1968) *[Photo by Father Luke]*

Page 102: 1968 Billikens Soccer, Defending NCAA Co-Champions, The University News (27 September 1968)

1969

1969 BILLIKENS SOCCER CLUB SCHEDULE

DATE	OPPONENT	NICKNAME	PLACE	SLU	OPPONENT
20 Sept.	Alumni		Musial Field	2	1
25 Sept.	West Berlin		Musial Field	3	1
27 Sept.	SLCC-Flo Valley	Magic	Musial Field	2	0
4 Oct.	Northern Illinois	Huskies	Dekalb, IL	8	0
11 Oct.	Rockhurst	Hawks	Musial Field	6	1
18 Oct.	Quincy	Hawks	Musial Field	2	1
25 Oct.	Michigan State	Spartans	E. Lansing, MI	2	0
1 Nov.	Washington Univ	Bears	Musial Field	8	0
8 Nov.	South Florida	Bulls	Tampa, FL	3	1
22 Nov.	SIUE	Cougars	Musial Field	4	0
29 Nov.	Cleveland State	Vikings	Musial Field	2	1
4 Dec.	Harvard	Crimson	San Jose, CA	2	1
6 Dec.	Univ of San Francisco	Dons	San Jose, CA	4	0

1969 SLU Championship Soccer Team. Row 1 (L-R): Jack Galmiche, John Pisani, Mike Seerey, Chuck Zoeller, Gene Geimer, Jim Leeker. **Row 2:** Steve Frank, Joe Hamm, Bill McDermott, Ed Neusel, Tim Flynn, Jim Niehoff. **Row 3:** Assistant coach Val Pelizzaro, Trainer Bob Albus, Al Trost, Don Copple, Pat Leahy, Gary Rensing, Head coach Harry Keough, Manager Pat Maloney.

In 1969, the Billikens came out of the gates and dominated, sailing to a 9-0-0 regular season record while outscoring their opponents 36-5. SLU began the NCAA Tournament facing their new archrival Southern Illinois University-Edwardsville (SIUE), their soon-to-be annual opponent in the Bronze Boot game. SIUE was also the host of the final tournament games. The Billikens sent the SIUE Cougars packing with a 4-0 loss, marched past their second round opponent, Cleveland State 2-1, and squeaked by undefeated Harvard 2-1 in a very close match. The team faced a tough San Francisco side, but managed to dominate the second half to beat the Dons 4-0 for their seventh national championship, achieving a truly perfect season, the second in the short history of the program. The sturdy defense was led by its two center backs, Steve Frank and Gary Rensing, who were each three-year starters. Al Trost led the team in scoring with 11 goals, was selected to the All-American team and was the recipient of the Hermann Trophy, the award given to the top college soccer player in the nation.

SIDELINE:
KEOUGH'S RIVALS

During Harry Keough's run as head coach from 1967 through 1973, there was an abundance of good competition for his teams. The number of quality college teams was constantly growing and it was not easy to single out those who might be considered "special" opponents of SLU during that time. Of particular note was Michigan State and Quincy College. Both teams' rosters included many St. Louis area players. Other competitors of note were UCLA, Howard and Southern Illinois University-Edwardsville.

Page 105 top: SLU Billiken vs SIU Cougars at Musial Field in St. Louis. SLU's Mike Seerey shoots while surrounded by SIU defenders during the final of the NCAA Midwest Tournament. SLU defeats SIU, 4-0 (22 November 1969) *[Photographer unknown]*

Page 105 bottom: SLU Billikens vs West Berlin University. SLU's John Pisani (on left) jumps for a headball alongside Jim Leeker (#21), as Al Trost (far right) looks on (25 September 1969) *[Photo by Father Luke]*

Page 106 top: SLU Billikens vs SIU-Edwardsville at Musial Field in St. Louis, MO. (22 November 1969) *[Photo by Father Luke]*

Page 106 bottom: SLU Men's Soccer. SLU All-American, Al Trost, volleys a shot on goal. (1969) *[Excerpted from 1970 Archive yearbook, page 180. Photographer unknown.]*

Page 107 top: SLU Billikens vs West Berlin University. Jim Leeker heads while John Pisani (L) and Gene Geimer look on (25 September 1969)

Page 107 bottom: SLU Billikens vs West Berlin University. John Pisani attacks in the penalty area (25 September 1969)

Page 108 top left: SLU Billikens vs SIU-Edwardsville at Musial Field in St. Louis. SLU's Jim Leeker heads the ball as Al Trost (left) and Pat Leahy (right) await the cross pass. (22 November 1969) *[Photo by Father Luke]*

Page 108 bottom left: SLU Billikens vs SIU-Edwardsville at Musial Field in St. Louis, MO. SLU's Mike Seerey dribbles the ball (22 November 1969) *[Photo by Father Luke]*

Page 109 top: SLU Billikens vs Flo. Valley (St. Louis Community College) at Musial Field in St. Louis, MO. Al Trost shoots, while Joe Hamm, Jim Leeker and Joe Leeker look on. (27 September 1969) *[Photo by Father Luke]*

Page 109 bottom: SLU Billikens vs Flo. Valley (St. Louis Community College) at Musial Field in St. Louis, MO as John Pisani heads into the penalty area. SLU defender Jim Niehoff is in the background (27 September 1969) *[Photo by Father Luke]*

Page 110 top: SLU Billiken vs SIU Cougars at Musial Field in St. Louis. SLU's Gene Geimer battles an SIU player for the ball during the final game of the NCAA Midwest Tournament. John Pisani (on left) and Pat Leahy (on right) trail behind. SLU wins 4 to 0. (22 November 1969) *[Photographer unknown; original image from SLU Sports Information Office]*

Page 111: Program for the 1969 NCAA Soccer Semi-Finals, SLU vs Colorado College. (4 December 1969) [Hosted and published by San Jose State College, California. Program courtesy of Jim Leeker.]

Page 112: A signed program from the soccer banquet at the end of the 1969 season (1969) [Program courtesy of Jim Leeker]

1969 SOCCER CHAMPIONSHIP

Spartan Stadium

SAN JOSE, CALIFORNIA

HOST

SAN JOSE STATE COLLEGE

SEMI-FINALS	FINALS
THURSDAY	SATURDAY
DECEMBER 4, 1969	DECEMBER 6, 1969
7:00 P.M.	1:30 P.M.
9:00 P.M.	

Program

[autograph: Stan Musial]

[autographs: Bob Bauman, Larry Hausmann]

OPENING REMARKS   LAWRENCE K. ALBUS

MVP PRESENTATION   HARRY KEOUGH

SPECIAL SERVICE PRESENTATION   VAL PELIZZARO

PLAYER PRESENTATION   STEVE FRANK

SPECIAL REMARKS   REV. PAUL C. REINERT, S.J.

[autographs: Dave Jokerst, Val Pelizzaro "Dukes", Harry Keough, Don Range, Russ Murphy, John Klein, Mike Houlihan, Bill O'Brien, Dan Avrrielli, Bob Kehoe, Wally Herra, Jay Moore, Sal Grasso, Thomas J. Trost, Paul Pisani]

1970

1970 BILLIKENS SOCCER CLUB SCHEDULE

DATE	OPPONENT	NICKNAME	PLACE	SLU	OPPONENT
19 Sept.	Saint Joseph's	Hawks	Philadelphia, PA	4	0
21 Sept.	Rider	Broncs	Lawrenceville, NJ	6	0
25 Sept.	Air Force Academy	Falcons	Musial Field	3	0
3 Oct.	St. Louis Stars		Musial Field	4	2
10 Oct.	Rockhurst	Hawks	Kansas City, MO	3	0
13 Oct.	Eastern Illinois	Panthers	Musial Field	5	0
17 Oct.	Quincy	Hawks	Quincy, IL	0	0
24 Oct.	South Florida	Bulls	Tampa, FL	5	1
25 Oct.	British Columbia	Thunderbirds	Musial Field	5	1
31 Oct.	Indiana Univ	Hoosiers	Musial Field	8	0
7 Nov.	SIUE	Cougars	Edwardsville, IL	3	1
21 Nov.	Akron Univ	Zips	Edwardsville, IL	7	0
28 Nov.	SIUE	Cougars	Edwardsville, IL	2	1
3 Dec.	Hartwick	Hawks	Edwardsville, IL	1	0
5 Dec.	UCLA	Bruins	Edwardsville, IL	1	0

1970 SLU Championship Soccer Team. Row 1 (L-R): Mike Seerey, Jim Draude, Jim Bokern, Mark Demling, Joe Leeker, Ed Neusel, Al Trost, Denny Hadican, John Eilerman, Jim Guttmann, Mike Finnegan, Denny Werner. **Row 2**: Manager Pete Maguire, Bill Gonzalez, Tim Flynn, Tom Torretti, Joe Hamm, Jim Evans, Al Steck, Don Copple, Bob Matteson, Dan Counce, Pat Leahy, Mark Gogel, Assistant coach Val Pelizzaro and Head coach Harry Keough. Missing from photo: Mike Finnegan.

In the Fall of 1970, a stellar recruiting class arrived on campus for the Billikens. Recruits included Jim Bokern, Dan Counce, Mark Demling, Denny Hadican, Bob Matteson, Al Steck and Denny Werner. That group started or saw significant playing time from their freshman year on, winning three out of four NCAA titles in their four years at SLU.

During the 1970 season, the Billikens gave up only six goals, two of which came during an exhibition match with a professional team, the St. Louis Stars. SLU also posted ten shutouts—the most in Billiken single-season history. The team featured a robust defense and exceptional goalkeeping from Don Copple and Al Steck. But defense was not the only trait that marked this team. They also averaged over four goals per game and were in the middle of a 45-game undefeated streak. The team was loaded with freshmen starters, including the team's leading scorer, Dan Counce, who finished the season with 14 goals. SLU entered the NCAA Tournament as the number one ranked team in the nation. The Billikens, as usual, relied heavily on St. Louis native players while their opponent in the final, UCLA, was composed of foreign-born players, typical of many college teams at that time. But the Billikens prevailed in a close match, winning 1-0 and bringing home their eighth national title. The national title was also won close to home, with the final games being hosted for a second year in a row at Southern Illinois University-Edwardsville. Al Trost won a second consecutive Hermann Trophy that year, and Joe Hamm took home All-American honors.

MIDFIELD MEMORY:
THROUGHOUT THE YEARS

By Bill McDermott

In December 1969, after playing in the NCAA Final at Spartan Stadium in San Jose, California, where we beat Harvard in the semi and University of San Francisco in the final, I distinctly remember walking around the field trying to take it all in. I knew this was my final game in college soccer and I was thinking I'd never be back on this field again.

Fast forward to April 1996 and the very first game in the new MLS at, believe it or not, Spartan Stadium in San Jose. I was the sideline reporter and my very first remarks were to the effect that it was a special date for me "because I haven't been on this field since December 1969 when I was a member of SLU's team and we won the NCAA Championship here." I get a call early the next week from one of my broadcast colleagues, Seamus Malin, to tell me that he was the assistant coach for

Harvard in the same Final Four and that he nearly fell off his chair when he heard my comments. I guess he was surprised that two of us from that game were announcing in the same league.

Another vivid memory I have is the very first time that I played soccer in the St. Philip Neri schoolyard with Don Ceresia. You see, Don would drive some of us from the neighborhood to his games at Fairgrounds Park and that very first image I saw of Fairgrounds #1 with the tarp around it is forever etched in my memory. To be able to watch all the players I had heard and read about, especially Don, who was from my neighborhood, solidified my aspiration to become part of the SLU team. I had offers from other schools but knew I wanted to go to SLU. And, without question, my first role model was Don Ceresia.

Which brings me to the phone call from Bob Guelker that I received in 1966 when I was a senior at McBride High School at our home on Claxton

Avenue in Walnut Park. It began with, "Billy, this is Bob Guelker and I'd like you to play soccer for me at Saint Louis University." To this day, that's all I remember of the conversation.

I suppose one of my favorite memories was after I graduated. I was at the Orange Bowl in Miami, Florida for the NCAA Final between SLU and UCLA in December 1972. SLU had beaten Howard in the semi—the same team they had lost to in the 1971 final. I was there as a representative of SLU and the Athletic Department and was to report back to KMOX Radio with game updates. It was also my very first meeting with the sometime acerbic reporter, Paul Gardner, who was bemoaning the fact that a team of Americans certainly couldn't win a National Championship, stating "they couldn't win last year, why should this year be any different?" Well, after a 4-2 win over UCLA, it gave me pride to bark at him, "Not only are we all American players, we're all from St. Louis!"

SIDELINE:

SLU COMES THROUGH

During the championship years, the players were not given any special memento to acknowledge their team's championship success. The reason likely was rooted in the fact that success was expected and as a result somewhat taken for granted. It took more than a few years, but SLU, beginning in 2000 with the 1959 Championship team, has annually awarded each player on the ten championship teams with a ring to acknowledge their collective achievement.

Page 115: SLU Billikens vs Hartwick College Hawks at the NCAA Soccer Semifinals at SIU-Edwardsville Field. SLU's Ed Neusel battles Hartwick in the first half. The Bills won 1-0, advancing them to the championship game against UCLA. (3 December 1970) *[Photographer unknown]*

Page 116: SLU Billikens vs UCLA in Edwardsville, IL.

SLU's (L-R) Pat Leahy, Tom Torretti, Joe Leeker and Bill Gonzalez, cheer on their teammates from the sidelines. (5 December 1970) *[Photographer credit: Bob Kolbrener and Lewis Portnoy]*

Page 117 top: SLU Billikens vs UCLA Bruins at SIU-Edwardsville. SLU's Mike Seerey is congratulated by Jim Bokern, Joe Hamm, Denny Werner, and

Dan Counce after the winning goal was scored. (5 December 1970) *[Excerpted from 1971 Archive yearbook, page 11. Photographer unknown.]*

Page 117 bottom: SLU Men's Soccer. SLU's Joe Leeker (#13) battles for the ball. Al Trost (left) and Mark Demling help defend. (1970) *[Excerpted from 1971 Archive yearbook, page 111. Photographer unknown.]*

Page 118: SLU Billikens vs. UCLA at SIU-Edwardsville. Denny Hadican celebrates after scoring the only goal in the 1970 Championship final victory over UCLA. (1972) *[Original photo from SLU Sports Information Office]*

Page 120: SLU Billikens vs Hartwick in Edwardsville, IL. Billiken Denny Werner (on left) dribbles the ball

away from a Hartwick defender. (3 December 1970) *[Excerpt of photo from SLU Sports Information Office, Photographer unknown]*

Page 121: SLU All-American, Joe Hamm (circa 1970)

Page 122: Billikens Win 8th National Title, The University News (11 December, 1970)

Billikens Win Eighth National Title

By MIKE GOEKE
Sports Editor

Well, they've done it again. The Billikens have walked off with the 1970 National Collegiate Athletic Association soccer championship, their eighth since Athletic Director Bob Stewart inaugurated soccer on a varsity level in 1959. The Bills have dominated soccer since then more than any school has dominated any college sport since Bud Wilkinson dominated the football world.

The Bills, under the guidance of Coach Harry Keough and assistant coach Val Pelizarro, shut out 10 of their fourteen opponents this season, and even beat the professional team in town, the St. Louis Stars, 4-2, outplaying them in the bargain. The only team they failed to beat, Quincy, really failed to threaten the Billiken goal, but it was just a matter of the Bills not being able to penetrate past the goalie. They outshot the Hawks 42-6.

The Bills trailed in only one game all year, and that was against SIU-Edwardsville, who briefly held a 1-0 lead over the Bills in the fourth quarter of the Midwest championships, before the Bills came back to score two goals, the last with only 10 seconds remaining in the game.

THE BILLS TAKE IT ALL

The game Saturday proved much closer than casual observation of the games Thursday would have predicted. UCLA had a great deal of trouble in beating Howard, and played more of a wide open game, scoring a lot of goals, but giving up pretty many also. It seemed that the Bills, who beat a tough Hartwick team, 1-0, in the next game, seemed to have the necessary ingredients to give the Bruins a sound drubbing.

However, the Bruins, a well coached and flexible squad, changed their style of play for the Billikens. They moved the ball deliberately, trying to set up their two high scorers, but the staunch Billiken defense turned in its usual brilliant game, and the Bruins failed to score.

Ed Neusel played perhaps the best game of his career, playing flawlessly. He handled every defensive assignment he was required to, and a few others besides. Don Copple was also required to make many tough stops, and he came through with one of his best games of the year.

Offensively, the Bills were hurt greatly by the strong wind, which hurt them both ways. One of their favorite plays is to hit one of their strikers, either Dan Counce or Mike Seerey, as he breaks past the defense. However, the wind either held the ball up too much, or blew the ball too far. In either case, it proved ineffective.

The sole scoring play in the game came in the third quarter when Mike Seerey put a long cross into the middle which eluded the UCLA goalie, and Denny Hadican headed it into the nets at the 11 minute mark. That proved to be all the Bills needed to bring home the championship.

THE PLAYERS

The Bills have been led all year by the unbelievable Al Trost, who has kept the middle under control for the Bills all year. When a team can have the kind of control that he and Joe Hamm have provided in the middle this year, the team can put relentless pressure on the opposition defense, which normally results in more goals for the Bills.

Up front, a number of different players have combined to bring success for the Bills. At striker, Counce and Seerey have been teaming up when Seerey has been healthy, with Hadican subbing for Seerey when knee trouble affected him during the latter half of the season before the playoffs.

On the wings, Jim Draude and Joe Leeker saw the most action, and played very well. Subbing for them was Jim Bokern and Hadi-

Mike Seerey, on ground, being congratulated on score against Hartwick.

can for the most part, with Jim Guttman seeing some action.

At linkman, as mentioned above, Trost and Hamm saw the most action, with Pat Leahy coming in to spell them frequently.

Probably the most surprising and encouraging part of the Billiken machine was the backfield. Three freshmen started in the backfield, along with senior stalwart Ed Neusel. These fellows were Denny Werner, Mark Demling, and Bob Matteson. The

very fact that they beat out many upperclassmen for the job was unbelievable, but more unbelievable was their play, which was almost as exciting as that of last year's backfield stalwarts, Gary Rensing and Steve Frank, and equally as aggressive.

Backing them up were Jimmy Evans and Tim Flynn, as well as freshman Tom Torretti.

The play in goal was in one word fantastic. Don Copple turned in many great games, culminating in the finals against UCLA. Backing him up was freshman Al Steck, who will likely be the

starting goalie next year, Copple is graduating.

Also graduating are Trost, N sel, and Joe Leeker, as well Evans, and Mark Gogel. The be missed, especially Trost Neusel, who will likely get offers. Leeker and Copple also get bids.

However, as can easily be se Coach Keough has so many g underclassmen coming back t he should be able to fill the h left by graduation, plus the that he has a number of fine p pects who are presently in h school. The Bills should domin for years to come.

Neusel flies to head ball away from UCLA offense.

Hadican drives past Hartwick defender.

1971

1971 BILLIKENS SOCCER CLUB SCHEDULE

DATE	OPPONENT	NICKNAME	PLACE	SLU	OPPONENT
4 Sept.	Alumni		Musial Field	2	1
11 Sept.	UMSL	Rivermen	Musial Field	2	1
18 Sept.	Wooster	Fighting Scots	Cleveland, OH	7	0
19 Sept.	Cleveland State	Vikings	Cleveland, OH	5	2
25 Sept.	Murray State	Racers	Musial Field	11	0
29 Sept.	MacMurray College	Highlanders	Musial Field	9	1
2 Oct.	Wheaton College	Crusaders	Wheaton, IL	3	0
5 Oct.	Eastern Illinois	Panthers	Charleston, IL	2	0
9 Oct.	Rockhurst	Hawks	Musial Field	4	0
16 Oct.	Quincy	Hawks	Musial Field	2	0
23 Oct.	South Florida	Bulls	Tampa, FL	4	1
30 Oct.	Northern Illinois	Huskies	Dekalb, IL	5	1
6 Nov.	SIUE	Cougars	Musial Field	2	1
20 Nov.	Illinois-Chicago	Dragons	Chicago, IL	4	1
27 Nov.	Ohio	Bobcats	Edwardsville, IL	4	0
4 Dec.	SIUE	Cougars	Edwardsville, IL	3	1
30 Dec.	San Francisco	Gators	Miami, FL	3	2
30 Dec.	Howard	Bison	Miami, FL	2	3

1971 SLU Soccer Team. Row 1 (L-R): Manager Pete Maguire, Joe Hamm, Mike Finnegan, Jim Bokern, Tim Logush, Tom Torretti, Jim Draude, John Eilerman, Denny Werner, Mark Demling, Bruce Hudson, Jim Guttmann. **Row 2:** Coach Harry Keough, Assistant coach Val Pelizzaro, Pat Leahy, Bob O'Leary, Dan Counce, Al Steck, Bob Herleth, Tim Flynn, Mike Seerey, Dale Harmon, Doug De Sa Queen, Bob Matteson, Denny Hadican, Trainer Bill Strecker.

SLU continued their success into the 1971 season winning by 16 straight games, including an 11-0 thrashing of Murray State, en route to the NCAA final. Their final opponent, Howard, featured a large number of foreign-born players and it was a close game. Howard prevailed 3-2 in a disappointing loss for the Billikens. The Howard Bisons were later disqualified and their national title taken away for using players that were ineligible to play. For that year only, the NCAA awarded no national title. Mike Seerey led the team in goals that season with 24, was named an All-American, and won the Hermann Trophy. 1971 was also the year that the Bronze Boot game was established, an annual match between local soccer powerhouses, Saint Louis University and Southern Illinois University-Edwardsville.

MIDFIELD MEMORY:

1971

By Mike Seerey

Two special memories…

It was October 23, 1971, and we were playing the University of South Florida in Tampa. We won the game 4-1. I scored a goal and assisted on another. After the game, we celebrated in our on-campus barracks room. The Northsiders competed against the Southsiders in a "beverage" chugging contest which we, the Northsiders, handily won. I was on the winning team twice that day—and it was my 21st birthday!

It was my Junior year and we were

playing SIU at Musial Field. As I was leaving the house, my Dad asked me if I was going to score a goal—a question he asked me all the time. I told him I was going to score at the parking lot end of the field. With under five minutes to go in the game, I caught the SIU goalie playing off his line and hit a half volley over his head for the game winner—at the parking lot end of the field. Of course I was only kidding about the parking lot end of the field thing, but you should have seen the grin on my Dad's face!

Page 125 top: SLU Billikens vs SIU Edwardsville in Edwardsville, IL. SLU's Mike Seerey fights for ball control as Jim Bokern (#7) and Bob O'Leary (on right) look on. (7 December 1971) [Photographer unknown]

Page 125 bottom: SLU Billikens vs SIU-E in Edwardsville, IL. SLU All-American, Bruce Hudson, shoots on goal as Dan Counce (on right) comes in to help. (1971) [Photographer unknown]

Page 126 & 127: SLU Billikens vs SIU-E in Edwardsville, IL. SLU fans hoist Jim Draude (left) and Head Coach Harry Keough (on right) on their shoulders after a Billiken win over SIU-E. (7 December 1971) [Photo by Globe-Democrat photographer, Dick Weddle.]

Page 128 top: SLU Billikens vs SIU-E at Edwardsville, IL. SLU's Bruce Hudson makes a tackle as Pat Leahy (on right) supports the play. (7 December 1971) [Photograph by Dick Weddle of the Globe-Democrat; original photo from SLU Sports Information Office]

Page 128 bottom left: SLU All-American, Bob Matteson, shields the ball from a defender. (1971) [Photographer unknown]

Page 128 bottom right: SLU Billikens vs Alumni at Musial Field in St. Louis. SLU's Tim Flynn

settles the ball as Bob Matteson stands by to assist. (4 September 1971) [Original slide from SLU Sports Information Office. Photo by James Wallhermfechtel.]

Page 129 top: SLU Billikens vs SIU-Edwardsville at Musial Field in St. Louis. SLU's Tim Flynn defends against against an SIU-E player. (6 November 1971) [Photographer unknown; original photo from SLU Sports Information Office]

Page 130: Program for the NCAA championship playoff against Southern Illinois University. (4 December 1971) [Hosted and published by Southern Illinois University, Edwardsville. Program courtesy of Jim Leeker.]

25¢

N. C. A. A.

MIDWEST
SOCCER TOURNAMENT

1971

COUGAR FIELD

Southern Illinois University, Edwardsville, Ill.

SATURDAY, DECEMBER 4, 1971

CHAMPIONSHIP FINAL

Southern Illinois University, Edwardsville

——————VERSUS——————

ST. LOUIS UNIVERSITY

Winner of the SIU-SLU game will advance to the 4-team National NCAA Championship Semi-Finals and final Dec. 28 and Dec. 30 at the Orange Bowl in Miami. St. Louis University is the defending NCAA Champion and is seeking its third straight national championship.

1972

1972 BILLIKENS SOCCER CLUB SCHEDULE

DATE	OPPONENT	NICKNAME	PLACE	SLU	OPPONENT
9 Sept.	UMSL	Rivermen	St. Louis	0	1
16 Sept.	UW-Green Bay	Phoenix	Musial Field	1	0
19 Sept.	MacMurray College	Highlanders	Jacksonville, IL	11	0
23 Sept.	Air Force Univ	Falcons	Colorado Springs, CO	5	1
24 Sept.	Metropolitan St.		Denver, Co	7	0
25 Sept.	Washington	Huskies	Seattle, WA	0	0
26 Sept.	Seattle Pacific	Falcons	Seattle, WA	1	1
28 Sept.	San Francisco	Gators	San Francisco, CA	1	0
30 Sept.	San Francisco	Gators	San Francisco, CA	4	1
7 Oct.	Wheaton College	Crusaders	Musial Field	5	0
8 Oct.	Cleveland State	Vikings	Musial Field	4	1
14 Oct.	Rockhurst	Hawks	Kansas City, MO	3	0
21 Oct.	Quincy	Hawks	Quincy, IL	0	1
28 Oct.	South Florida	Bulls	Musial Field	1	0
5 Nov.	SIUE	Cougars	Busch Stadium	1	1
18 Nov.	Illinois-Chicago	Dragons	Musial Field	7	0
23 Nov.	Bowling Green	Falcons	Athens, OH	2	0
8 Dec.	Ohio	Bobcats	Athens, OH	3	1
27 Dec.	Howard	Bison	Miami, FL	2	1
29 Dec.	UCLA	Bruins	Miami, FL	4	2

1972 SLU Championship Soccer Team. Row 1 (L-R): Denny Werner, Bob Matteson, Joe Clarke, Denny Hadican, Tim Logush, Tom Torretti, Jim Bokern, Mike Seerey, Bob O'Leary, Jim Guttmann, John Eilerman, Tim Hoffman. **Row 2:** Assistant Coach Val Pelizzaro, Manager Pete Maguire, Mark Demling, Tom Neusel, Dan Counce, Dale Harmon, Bruce Hudson, Pat Leahy, Chuck Zorumski, Al Steck, Tom Pelizzaro, Joe Hamm, Head Coach Harry Keough.

The 1972 squad was not going to dwell on the memory of the previous year's final. SLU began its run for a ninth national title on Thanksgiving Day, the beginning of the NCAA Tournament. Leading up to the final, they lost only two games, each by one goal. Once in the tournament, they never looked back. After cruising through two victories, the semifinal game saw a rematch of last year's title game against Howard. This time, it was the Billiken's time to win. They scored 8:37 into sudden death overtime. The 1972 final was a rematch of the 1970 championship, pitting SLU against UCLA. Despite a brawl which emptied both benches, stopped the game for 15 minutes and left two Billikens injured, SLU prevailed 4-2 over the Bruins for the national championship. Mike Seerey led the team in scoring again, this year with 14 goals, and won his second consecutive Hermann Trophy.

SIDELINE:

NORTH VS. SOUTH

To most Americans, if they heard the phrase "North vs. South," they would immediately recall the American Civil War where the Union and Confederate armies bloodied each other in the early 1860s. In the context of Saint Louis University soccer, "North vs. South" had a slightly different meaning. For the SLU player, on game day you were first and foremost a SLU player. In practice games, however, those SLU players were divided into Northside and Southside camps who would vie for supremacy and the accompanying bragging rights. The Northsiders came from the Catholic parishes in north St. Louis City and St. Louis County, such as St. Phillip Neri, and the Southsiders from south St. Louis parishes, such as Immaculate Heart of Mary. There was always an ebb and flow to this competition. One year the Northsiders played a bit better and the next year the Southsiders had the edge. While friendly, the competition between the two camps was always intense, and the debate never ended.

Page 133 top: SLU Billiken Soccer player, Joe Clarke, played with the team from 1972 through 1975 seasons. He returned as coach from 1983 through 1996. This photo was taken in 1974 during Clarke's Junior year. *[Courtesy of SLU Sports Information]*

Page 133 bottom: SLU VS Bowling Green in Athens, OH in the semi-final NCAA Midwest Tournament. SLU's Mike Seerey settles the ball, flanked by Joe Hamm (on left) and Dan Counce [#9]. The Billikens defeated Bowling Green 2-0. (23 November 1972) *[Photographer unknown]*

Page 134 top left: SLU Billikens vs UCLA Bruins at the Orange Bowl in Miami, FL. Coach Harry Keough and Mike Seerey hold the 1972 NCAA Championship Trophy. (29 December 1972) *[Photographer unknown]*

Page 134 bottom left: SLU Billikens vs Howard University in the 1972 NCAA semi-final in Miami, FL. The Bills fight for ball control, L-R: Bruce Hudson, Joe Hamm, Dan Counce and Denny Werner. SLU defeats Howard University 2-1. (27 December 1972) *[Photographer unknown; original photo from SLU Sports Information Office]*

Page 135 top: SLU Billikens vs UCLA Bruins at the Orange Bowl in Miami, FL. The Bills congratulate one another after securing the 1972 NCAA championship, listed L-R: Joe Hamm, Mike Seerey, Dan Counce, Al Steck (goalie), and Joe Clarke. (29 December 1972) *[Photographer unknown]*

Page 135 bottom: SLU Billikens vs UCLA Bruins at the Orange Bowl in Miami, FL. SLU All-American, Mike Seerey, sprints with ball, beating out a UCLA defender. SLU wins 4-2. (29 December 1972) *[Photographer unknown]*

Page 136: SLU Billikens vs Cleveland State at Musial Field in St. Louis. SLU's Jim Bokern scores on a penalty kick in a 4-1 SLU victory. Teammates (L-R) Denny Werner, Pat Leahy, Bob O'Leary, Bob Matteson and Bruce Hudson look on. (8 October 1972) *[Original photo from SLU Sports Information Office; photographer unknown]*

1973

1973 BILLIKENS SOCCER CLUB SCHEDULE

DATE	OPPONENT	NICKNAME	PLACE	SLU	OPPONENT
8 Sept.	UMSL	Rivermen	Mullaly Field	3	3
13 Sept.	Springfield	Spirits	Florissant Valley	2	0
15 Sept.	Pennsylvania	Quakers	Philadelphia, PA	2	0
17 Sept.	U of Connecticut	Huskies	Storrs, Mansfield CT	2	1
20 Sept.	National Uruguay	Charruas	Mullaly Field	1	2
22 Sept.	Davis & Elkins	Senators	Quincy Tourn.	2	0
23 Sept.	West Virginia	Mountaineers	Quincy Tourn.	4	1
29 Sept.	Quincy	Hawks	Mullaly Field	5	2
6 Oct.	UW-Green Bay	Phoenix	Green Bay, WI	0	1
8 Oct.	Cleveland State	Vikings	Cleveland, OH	1	1
13 Oct.	Rockhurst	Hawks	Mullaly Field	2	1
27 Oct.	South Florida	Bulls	Tampa, FL	2	1
29 Oct.	Rollins	Tars	Orlando, FL	3	1
3 Nov.	SIUE	Cougars	Busch Stadium	1	0
17 Nov.	Illinois Chicago	Dragons	Chicago, IL	0	0
19 Nov.	American	Eagles	Mullaly Field	1	0
24 Nov.	Bowling Green	Falcons	Edwardsville, IL	6	0
9 Dec.	SIUE	Cougars	Busch Stadium	3	0
1 Jan.	Brown	Brown Bears	Orange Bowl	3	1
4 Jan.	UCLA	Bruins	Orange Bowl	2	1

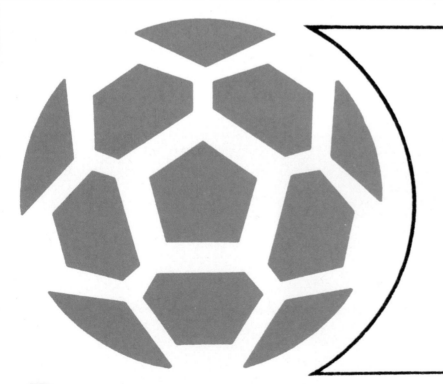

Billiken Soccer 1973

SLU continued their winning ways through the 1973 season. They entered the NCAA Tournament once again with a number one ranking while achieving a 12-2-3 record. The team earned the top spot after defeating Southern Illinois University-Edwardsville in the annual Bronze Boot game. The NCAA final pitted SLU against UCLA for the second consecutive year and the third time in four years. In a closely contested game, the Billikens outshot the Bruins 34-12, but needed overtime to send UCLA home without the title. Following the season, seven Billiken seniors were drafted into the North American Soccer League, including four in the first round. Dan Counce led the team with 11 goals that year and won the Hermann Trophy, making it five years in a row that a SLU player was named the top college soccer player in the nation. That year Joe Hamm and Mike Seerey, along with former Billiken Al Trost, were all named to the Olympic team.

1973 SLU Championship Soccer Team. Row 1 (L-R): Bob Matteson, Bruce Rudroff, Kevin Handlan, John Roeslein, Jim Bokern, Tom Torretti, Tom Neusel, Tom Renaud, Jim Guttmann, and Denny Hadican. Row 2: Dan Flynn, Mark Demling, Don Droege, Tim Hoffman, Bruce Hudson, Denny Werner, Joe Clarke, Tom Pelizzaro, Dan Counce, Tim Logush. **Row 2:** Assistant Coach Miguel de Lima, Head Coach Harry Keough, Len Deschler, Bob Herleth, Al Steck, Chuck Zorumski, Jaime Vargas, Assistant Coach Val Pelizzaro.

MIDFIELD MEMORY:

SOCCER TRIP TO CHILE

By Mark Demling

Landing in Santiago, Chile in August 1973 was eye-opening. The government was in upheaval. There was a transportation strike, and cars were lined for miles at the gas stations.

The army was everywhere. Going through customs at the airport we spotted a huge pool of blood on the ground as we passed security gates. We were picked up by a U.S. Embassy bus to transport us to the local club where we were playing. We went by the Presidential palace where there was a tank outside the gates. Bullet holes were numerous on the palace walls. That

night we were playing indoor soccer in the club's gym at the complex where we stayed. The President was about to give a speech on radio or television. The rebels blew up a huge electronic tower and blacked out the entire city. We didn't know what happened until the next morning.

SIDELINE:

THE GOLDEN AGE OF ST. LOUIS SOCCER

This book, of course, is devoted to the glories Saint Louis University attained during the period of 1959 to 1973. The successes of SLU were a product of the fertile St. Louis soccer fields where talent was abundant. SLU, however, was not the only St. Louis success story during that period.

If you go back to 1950, St. Louis area teams dominated the U.S. soccer landscape on many levels. At the Junior Cup level (now the U-19 year old category), between 1956 and 1984, St. Louis teams won the national title 19 times out of a possible 29 titles. On the men's senior level, St.

Louis teams earned six national titles in the Amateur Cup and the Open Cup title in 1957. In addition, Kutis won it again in 1971, and Busch prevailed a year later in 1972. On the junior college level, Florissant Valley, under Coach Pete Sorber, won seven national titles. Meramec Community College also won a title in 1972. Finally, on the college level, Southern Illinois University at Edwardsville (SIUE) and the University of Missouri at St. Louis (UMSL) always fielded excellent teams with SIUE winning the first Division II national title in 1972 and UMSL taking the title in 1973. Other Midwest colleges such as Quincy College, Rockhurst, and St. Benedict's College—all NAIA teams—had very good teams during this era, with substantial numbers of their players being from St. Louis.

The pinnacle year of St. Louis soccer supremacy, at least on the college level, was 1973 when SLU won the Division I NCAA title, UMSL won the Division II title, Quincy won the NAIA crown, and Florissant Valley won the junior college championship. It should also be noted that Rockhurst and Meramec each lost the NAIA and Division II title games respectively. Furthermore, SIUE, which lost to SLU in the NCAA Tournament, finished second to the Billikens in the final Coaches' Poll rankings. SLU was ranked first, SIUE second, and UMSL fifth.

The degree of dominance of the St. Louis area and teams fueled by St. Louis talent was staggering. It is unlikely we will ever again see that kind of domination on all levels of men's college soccer by a single city.

Page 138 bottom: SLU Billiken pocket schedule (1973) *[Courtesy of the SLU Sports Information Office]*

Page 139 top: SLU Billikens Men's Soccer. John Roeslein looks to trap the ball. (circa 1973) *[Scanned from 1974 SLU Soccer Media Guide, page 14. Photographer unknown.]*

Page 140 & 141: SLU Billikens vs Sante Fe Reserves in Bogota, Colombia. The Billiken Soccer Team carries the Columbian flag prior to their match with the Sante Fe Reserves in Bogota, Colombia--the first stop on the 1973 South American Tour. Line of players on the left: Jim Bokern, Denny Werner, Dan Counce, Al Steck, Don Droege, Dan Flynn, and Kevin Handlan. Line of players on right: Bob Matteson, Pat Leahy, Chuck Zorumski, Bruce Hudson, Joe Clarke, Bruce Rudroff, Len Deschler, and John Roeslein (1973). *[Photographer unknown; original photo from SLU Sports Information Office]*

Page 142: SLU Billikens vs Rockhurst at Mullaly Field in St. Louis. The Billiken's Bob Matteson (left) keeps a Rockhurst defender off-balance in a 2-1 SLU victory. (13 October 1973) *[Scan of photo from SLU Sports Information Office, Photo by James Wallhermfechtel]*

Page 143 top left: SLU All-American, Don Droege (1973) *[Photographer unknown; original image from SLU Sports Information Office]*

Page 143 top right: SLU Billikens vs UMSL at Francis Field in St. Louis. SLU All-American, Joe Clarke (middle), pushes through two UMSL players to head the ball. (6 September 1975) *[Photo courtesy of SLU Sports Information]*

Page 143 bottom left: Dan Counce, SLU All-American, scores the winning goal against the SIU-Edwardsville Cougars. (9 December 1973) *[Photographer unknown; original magazine photo from SLU Sports Information Office]*

Page 143 bottom right: SLU Soccer All-American, Bruce Rudroff (1973) *[Image of slide from SLU Sports Information Office]*

Page 144 top: SLU Billikens vs UCLA Bruins in the NCAA Final. SLU's Jim Bokern (#7) and Bob Matteson look to control the ball. (1973) *[Photographer unknown, scan of original photo from SLU Sports Information Office]*

Page 144 bottom: SLU Billikens vs SIUE at Busch Stadium in St. Louis. SLU's Jim Bokern (left) traps

the ball as John Roeslein (#8) stands ready to assist. (9 November 1973) *[Original photo from SLU Sports Information Office. Photo by James Wallhermfechtel.]*

Page 145: SLU Billikens vs UCLA in the 1973 NCAA Final. SLU's Bruce Hudson and John Roeslein attempt a shot on goal. (4 January 1974) *[Photographer unknown; original photo from SLU Sports Information Office]*

Page 146: We're Number One! (Photos), The University News, November 16, 1973

CONCLUSION

Page 147: SLU Billikens vs. UCLA at SIU-Edwardsville. Denny Hadican celebrates after scoring the only goal in the 1970 Championship final victory over UCLA. (1972) *[Original photo from SLU Sports Information Office]*

Page 148: Soccer Bills Capture 10th NCAA Title, The University News, January 18, 1974

THE UNIVERSITY NEWS

VOL. 53, No. 10

Friday, November 16, 1973

We're Number One!

CONCLUSION

Saint Louis University's championship run ended in 1973. The 1974 season saw SLU lose in the NCAA Division I championship game to Howard 2-1 in overtime. The game could have gone either way, and with a different bounce of the ball here or there, it could have been 11 championships in 16 years. The reasons for the end of the championship run are many. The primary factor is that the rest of the United States, beginning in the late 1960s, had slowly began to grasp,

and would eventually embrace, the love of soccer that the St. Louis area had long known. Youth soccer was becoming much more popular across the country at the grassroots level, and the number of high schools and colleges fielding teams had increased dramatically. Not only were there more teams at all levels, the number of competitive teams was also skyrocketing. Since 1973, SLU has continued to field excellent teams on the men's side, and now also on the women's. Since the last championship, the men's team has reached the final four on several occasions and still regularly participates in the NCAA Tournament. The real legacy of the

University's glorious 15-year run of championships and near misses is that SLU became an ambassador of the St. Louis soccer scene. The SLU teams, over many years, demonstrated to the rest of the U.S. that American kids who were well-schooled in the game, worked hard on the field and focused on playing as a team, could not only compete on the soccer pitch but also excel at the highest level. Saint Louis University can be very proud of its role in helping to put soccer on the map in the United States.

Soccer Bills Captur 10th NCAA Title

By Bob Herleth

UCLA, the kingpin of the basketball world, is the beholder of one of the most fantastic sports records. They have completely dominated the action on the hardwood for the past decade, in both regular season and tournament play. Before the season is over, they just might notch their 100th consecutive victory, a full 39 games better than the previous official NCAA record.

Nevertheless, there is another record that the Bruins of UCLA have participated in recently. This time the stage is the soccer field. The record is finishing second in the national tournament three out of the past four years—to the same team. The frequency of being a bridesmaid is at best an unofficial record, and is hardly the type of prestige a team is after. However, the frequency of the Billikens corralling the national championship is no fluke. It's official, they are the best. And if you think the kickers from L.A. have trouble sleeping, knowing they have lost three times to the same team in the NCAA finals, you are probably right.

In an exciting and climactic finish, SLU topped the UCLANS on January 4th, by the score of 2-1 in overtime. It brought their season's record to 13-1-3, which excludes three exhibition games they participated in during the regular season. Their official ledger also does not include the preseason tour of the South American continent throughout the month of August.

That's right, remember those 90-degree days prevalent in August? It was a whole month before semester one even began. And now, it's been barely two weeks since the soccer Billikens captured their tenth national championship out of a possible fifteen. Thus the efforts of the Bills have ranged from heat to cold, grass to snow, and even from continent to continent.

As in the past two years, the NCAA soccer championships have been held in conjunction with the Orange Bowl festivities. This year the participants included Brown and Clemson Universities, along with the already mentioned Billikens and Bruins. Each of them secured the right to play by a series of sectional playoff games. In the semifinal matches, it was Clemson vs. UCLA and Brown vs. SLU.

In the initial contest, the Bruins outlasted Clemson 2-1 in overtime. In the latter match, SLU thoroughly dominated the Eastern representative, and downed Brown University by a 3-1 margin.

Thus the stage was set for the championship game, to be played two days later. In 1970 the Billikens defeated the Bruins 1-0, and in 1972

Mark Demling heads the Bills out of trouble at the Orange Bowl

the margin was a 4-2 victory for the Bills. Strangers they were not, but rivals they were, as these two teams collided once again. SLU began the game in a very slow, and occasionally sloppy fashion. After only 4:24 into the game, UCLA jumped into an early lead on the strength of a goal by Firooz Fowzi. It was at least a partial gift however, since Fowzi was able to take advantage of a slight misplay between midfielder, Bob Matteson and goalie, Chuck Zorumski.

By the midway point of the first half, the Billikens began to dominate the offensive action. But it was not until ten minutes had elapsed in the second half when the Bills were able to knot the score. Forward, Dan Counce managed to slip inside the right upright, which then tied the score. Denny Hadican was credited with the assist.

The two squads battled scoreless for another 35 minutes to push the game into overtime. By this time, the superior conditioning of the soccer Bills began to pay off. Assistant coach, Val Pelizarro, deserves the credit in this department. As the minutes ticked away in the overtime session, there was little doubt which team would win. At 5:43 of the extra session, Dan Counce garnered his second tally of the day, when he picked up a loose ball in front of the net, and fired it into the cords.

In the numbers department, it is now ten of a possible 15 NCAA soccer championships for the school, 5 of 7 for head coach Harry Keough, and 3 of 4 for the graduating seniors. For the school and Coach Keough, there is the challenge of next year. For the seniors, they will leave knowing that they have done as well as any class previous to them. In many ways their feats of the past four years ought to rank at least a bit higher on the Billiken soccer scale. Today, there are not only more and more schools playing soccer, but there are also many more that now function on a competitive basis.

So the ever-growing soccer season is finally over. It is now the time for drafting, reflecting, and recruiting. With the rise of professional soccer, several seniors are anxious ing the outcome of the upco draft. Although the All- selection committee se overlook the talents of sev players, you can be sure professional talent scouts

The job of reflecting is th anyone who chooses to There are many topics wor flecting. Certainly the pla reflect in terms of thou miles. For awards coun Bills seem to have bee changed. Counce and Matte selected for the Senior B lando, Florida, and were corded honorable men America selection. Dan Co also be honored by the baseball writers for his tions to amateur soccer.

Finally, the job of recru be Coach Harry Keough with his assistants Val Peli Miguel deLima. Losing te including seven starters v easy to replace. But in pionship year of 1970, th four freshmen in the sta up, and Dennis Hadican Jim Bokern were top-serves.

Next year, it will be time the Billikens will try trio of national champio gether. In the 15-year Billiken soccer, this has done. But for the momen much sweetness in relishi that the soccer Bills are

Baseba

Tom Dix, Billiken basel announces that there will ing on Friday, February of those interested in pla ball this Spring. The me take place in the gym For the moment, the ten of the meeting is 4:00 p.

Fireline

The Fireline bus sy announced that they w service for all weeken events. The bus will b Griesedieck Hall an hou each home game. Servic tinue at 15 minute interv way up til game time.

Replay

For the benefit of all h who were out of town recent holiday break, rebroadcast the Billikens 2 victory over Minnes finals of the Fireman Hockey Tournament. The will be on Kbil at 6: Monday, January 21.